Decorating Tricks
Touches of Style

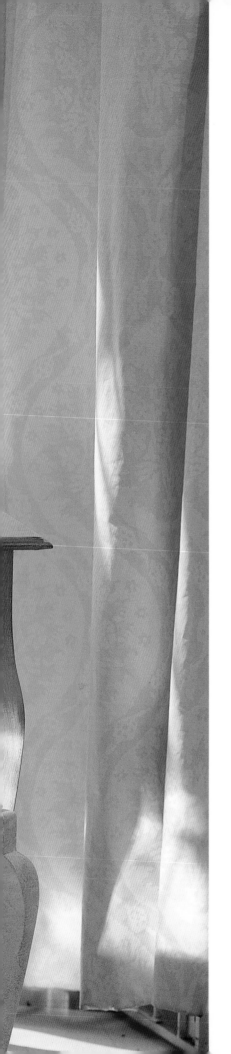

Decorating Tricks
Touches of Style

Over 40 quick-to-do projects,
from an hour to a weekend

Maggie Colvin

HAMLYN

First published in 1998 by Hamlyn
an imprint of Reed Consumer Books Limited
Michelin House, 81 Fulham Road
London, SW3 6RB
and Auckland and Melbourne

Publishing Director LAURA BAMFORD

Executive Editor MIKE EVANS
Senior Editor NINA SHARMAN
Managing Editor SUSIE BEHAR
Art Director KEITH MARTIN
Art Editor LOUISE GRIFFITHS
Designer VIVEK BHATIA
Production BONNIE ASHBY

Photography DI LEWIS
Illustrations CAROL HILL

A CIP record for this book is available
from the British Library.

ISBN 0 600 59423 8

The publishers have made every effort to ensure that
all instructions given in this book are accurate and
safe, but they cannot accept liability for any resulting
injury, damage or loss to either person or property
whether direct or consequential and howsoever
arising. The author and publishers will be grateful for
any information which will assist them in keeping
future editions up-to-date.

Produced by Toppan Printing Co Ltd
Printed and bound in China

Introduction	6
Basic tool kit	7
Botch-proof colour schemes	10

ONE-HOUR WONDERS 14

Party name places	16
Fabric sewing box	18
Fabric photo frame and pencil pots	20
Finger-painted tray	22
Paper lampshades	24

TWO-HOUR TRANSFORMATIONS 26

Flower vase frame	28
Handpainted and glazed terracotta ware	30
Frosted window with flowerpot stencils	32
Vinegar-painted frame	34
Picture frame candelabra	36

MORNING MAKEOVERS 38

Gustavian-style cupboard	40
Seersucker fan blind	42
Doll's-house cupboard	44
Window screen	46
Gustavian-style dressing table	48

Contents

Handpainted blind   50
Oriental bamboo frame   52
Antique-style console   54

EVENING ESCAPADES   56

Woodgrained and stencilled
     table top   58
Goblet-headed curtains   60
Trompe l'oeil kitchen
     dresser   62
Clover leaf shutters   66
Decoupage firescreen   68
Fake china cupboard
     with chicken wire   70
Stencilled pine chair   74
Coffee table stool   76

SAME-DAY SENSATIONS   78

Faux inlaid granite table top   80
Fake trellis doors   84
Faux marquetry table top   86
Office chair transformation   88
Mosaic table top   92
Sofa divan transformation   96
Fake inlaid marble   98
Tented shelving   102
Faux malachite with gold leaf   104
Marbled table top with
     malachite inlay   108

WEEKEND WONDERS   110

Lambrequin pelmet   112
Concealed cupboards   114
Stencilled bedlinen   116
Director's chair cover   118
Swedish sleigh bed   122
Sofa cover   124
Child's cabin bed   128
Bathroom makeover   130

INGENIOUS IDEAS   134

Decorative doors   136
Sheer delights   138
Floral tricks   140

Index   142
Acknowledgements   144

Introduction

In an ideal textbook world, everybody would work out a room-by-room perfect plan for their home before lifting a paintbrush or visiting the shops to make that fatal impulse purchase. From door handles to the position of wallplugs, halogen spotlights and colours, everything would work, relate and harmonize just like Pythagoras' theorem. Of course we instinctively know how sensible this is but also how hard it is to put it into action.

The reality is that most people don't know what they want until they see it in the shops or on a printed page. Real life is often about coping with a patterned carpet you hate, or a window overlooking that immovable brick wall, or the hideous sofa you would like to throw out, if only you could afford to.

When ingenuity and inspiration seem lacking, along with time, money and effort, it is often just the one original idea that can inspire you to action and set off a string of improvements which can ultimately transform a room. I have always believed that decorating is about small beginnings and hitting upon that one appropriate great idea that leads on to the next. So this book is essentially a collection of the best ideas I have collected that I believe to be inspired, extremely useful, fun to do and, most importantly, they all produce excellent visual results.

Achieving the correct colour scheme is vital in making a success of a decorating idea. I have devoted several pages to botch-proof colour schemes whose success, like well proven cookery recipes, have been tried and tested over the years. These colour schemes will always work, whether you apply them to a grand house or a cottage, to whole rooms or to small areas or items such as an arrangement of flowers. Where possible the colours I have used for projects are printed next to the project on the same page so that you can take them to the paint shop if you want to recreate results accurately.

None of the projects in this book require great skill or expense, and all of them are roughly timed to give an idea of the time commitment involved. The timing is only a rough indication and some projects may take longer. This is not necessarily because they are more complicated but where they involve painting, I have not included the drying times of paints or glazes. Any type of oil-based paint will add considerably to the overall timing of the project.

Many of my projects are all about turning junk into treasure which always creates a feeling of personal achievement, making any effort involved well worthwhile. This book covers many ideas that will not break the bank, and they all have staying power. The most brilliant aspect of the ideas is the scope they offer to create individual results. No two person's paint effects are ever quite the same. An analogy I would use as a comparison is that individually painted furniture is as different, interesting and special as home cooking is to shop-bought prepared meals.

But before you begin, here are some reminders of what is worth keeping in your tool cupboard. Having to rush to the shops to buy the odd bit of sandpaper is a hiccup which, apart from interrupting your artistic flow, will almost certainly waste time and energy that is best spent on the project in hand.

Maggie Colvin

Basic tool kit
equipment:

Measuring tape (1)
Carpenter's pencil (2)
Wire cutters (3)
Pair of compasses (4)
Fretsaw (5)
Jigsaw (6)

Electric drill (not shown)
Sandpaper (7)
Spirit level (8)
Scissors (9)
Scraper (10)
Wire brush (11)
Staple gun (12)
Screwdrivers (13)
Hammers (14)

Basic tool kit

Even the most sensibly stocked tool cupboard is unusable if you can't lay your hands on what you need in a few seconds. Inevitably this means labelling everything and having a place for everything and keeping everything in its place. I find it helpful to group equipment that you usually use for the same type of jobs and store it in well-labelled containers. Labels written directly on to the containers with thick marker pens tend to wear better than individual sticky labels which can fall off or wear away.

Basic painting
equipment:

Hot pen (for cutting
acetate) (1)
Dragging brush (2)
Stippling brush (3)
Stencil brushes (4)
Stencil paints (5)
Household paintbrushes (6)

Acetate (7)
Woodgrainer (8)
Stencil crayons (9)
Mutton (cheese) cloth (10)
Masking tape in different
widths (11)
Artist's acrylic colours (12)
Natural sponge (13)
Artist's brushes (14)
Softening brush (15)

7

10

8

9

11

14

15

When storing tools on shelves, if you have the choice, go for narrow shelves, as these are easier to keep in visual order than deep ones which can end up cluttered. Tools hung on a hook and outlined on a wall are easier to find than those stored in a box or placed in a jar. Everybody, of course, is free to evolve their own system. Experiment in order to find a particular system that suits you best.

Botch-proof colour schemes

Choosing colour is one of the most absorbing, fun and sumptuous aspects of interior design. Fortunately many people possess an innate colour sense. They file away and reproduce successful colour recipes, apparently without thinking. For other, less confident people, colour is such a powerful medium, so emotive and personal, that they find the choices daunting when deciding on colour schemes. Here is an attempt to demystify colour with some fail-safe recipes.

Although many excellent books have been written on the subject, the best way to learn and build up your own confidence with colour is through observation and practice. To cultivate your own colour sense and even just to find out what you like, you actually have to train yourself to use your eyes.

Try to recall the hotel foyer that you admired when you were on holiday, or a favourite restaurant or room in a stately home and analyse the colour ingredients. You could even make a note of them. Which colours and in what proportion did they comprise the total scheme? Was the overall impression of one dominating colour? Were they old-fashioned, slightly faded and greying colours, modern, clear and punchy, or more translucent pastels mixed with a white base? Colour recipes are no more complicated to understand than culinary recipes and, in the same way, they need sampling. Then, as

with recipes in a cookbook, once listed they are easy to reproduce.

Without delving too far into the science of colour, or the psychological aspects (everybody has a theory), here are some of the most reliable colour recipes which the professionals fall back on time and time again. Widely tried and tested, even throughout art history, they comprise what I describe as botch-proof colour schemes. If you are about to furnish a home or paint a piece of furniture and fear that you might make a mistake, these are very reliable starter packs.

NEUTRAL COLOUR SCHEMES

Nearly always based on white or off-white combined with grey, stone and buff colours, natural colour schemes can look extremely glamorous, especially if you add different textures to offset any blandness. For instance, choose wood and sisal or smooth, shiny marble or white tiles for floorings, natural wood for furniture combined with textured fabrics, and lush cotton tassels and fringing for soft furnishings. A variety of texture is vital. Once you have established the neutral background you can then add accents of colour. Limewashed furniture (see page 48), granite effects (see page 80), creamy marbling (see page 98) and fake pale wood effects (see page 58) fit into this category and will all blend in beautifully.

MONOCHROME COLOUR SCHEMES

Quite simply choose a colour, say green or terracotta, and work through different tones of that one shade. Add patterns in the same colour to liven it up and, if you choose a dark colour (see the dark green drawing room below), counterbalance this with a pale neutral shade for the floor. It will reflect light without detracting from the overall impression of green. A pale yellow base with a deeper yellow sponged effect (see page 68) and bright emerald green washed over a forest green (see page 122) are good examples of this colour scheme.

YOUR FAVOURITE COLOUR WITH WHITE

This may sound like a cliché but if you analyse the pages of home furnishing magazines, you will be amazed at the number of schemes based on this recipe. Blue and white is the all-time favourite, but yellow and white, and green and white are all immensely appealing. The overall effect will be fresh and uncomplicated. Obviously the exact choice of the one colour is all-important. Choose a baby blue and you have the basis of a pretty child's room. Select a violet-grey blue with a creamy white, as used in the bedroom shown here, and the end result is much more sophisticated and grown-up.

COMPLEMENTARY OR CONTRASTING COLOUR SCHEMES

Many professionals hardly ever appear to consult the colour wheel, but if you do not fall into this category then the wheel is invaluable for working out complementary schemes. The colour wheel is based on the natural colours found in the rainbow, where the best relationship of colours is to be discovered. The king-pin colours in the wheel are the three primaries, red, blue and yellow, and from these literally millions of different colours are derived. Secondary colours are an equal mix of the primaries and make orange, green and purple. Colours in between are called tertiary colours. For some reason – and nobody has really come up with a satisfactory explanation for the

fact – if you mix colours sitting opposite each other on the wheel, you will inevitably hit a happy mix. For instance, the blue and yellow colour scheme featured in the kitchen (right), is one of the world's best selling colour schemes. Subtle variations,

such as grey blue and gold, can be found in furnishings and even whole rooms in many of the grand houses in Europe.

When it comes to creating a distressed look for furniture contrasting colours work best. Some examples are dark forest

green painted on to antique red, covered first in wax, or blue-grey painted over coral, and so on.

When choosing colours for a whole room, a calmer more satisfactory result is achieved by ensuring one colour dominates and by avoiding a fifty-fifty mix

of two colours which can look a little uncomfortable.

ANALOGOUS COLOUR SCHEMES

These are calming harmonious schemes incorporating three or four colours that are adjacent on the colour wheel. For instance, the mixture of turquoise, dark blue and green used for the mosaic table top on page 92 is a good example. As these colours sit well together they make a useful choice for single piece of furniture, which in turn will need to be fitted into the larger visual context of a room. Used as the basis for a room colour scheme, a set of analogous colours often cries out for a contrasting colour, even just in a small dollop, to help put energy and life into the total scheme but sometimes just a background of white or off-white will do the same trick.

One-hour Wonders

Even one hour of creativity working with inexpensive materials can yield hugely satisfying results. These projects are simple enough for children to help with – especially the finger painting and party name places ideas. The lampshades and photo frames are mostly cut and stick jobs, and the fabric box is perfect for a first sewing project.

- ■ Party name places

- ■ Fabric sewing box

- ■ Fabric photo frame and pencil pots

- ■ Finger-painted tray

- ■ Paper lampshades

Party name places

Individual name places go a long way to make your party guests feel special and are particularly useful at large family or children's parties. Tiny terracotta pots with spray-painted names make original table accessories which can double up as candleholders or napkin holders, or be filled with chocolates or other goodies.

You will need:

Small terracotta pots
Glue gun and glue
Newspaper
Gold spray paint
Acrylic varnish

Small household paintbrush
Dry oasis (if used as a
 candleholder)
Candles (if used as a
 candleholder)
Dried moss

If you have never used a glue gun before, practise writing on a piece of card before you start on the pot. If you do not have access to a glue gun, plasticine rolled into long thin strips can be made into letters. When using spray paint, work in a well-ventilated room or outdoors .

1. Make sure the terracotta pot is clean and dry. Heat the glue in the glue gun and carefully write the name or initials of your guest on to the pot

2. When the glue is dry, place the pot on an old newspaper and spray with the gold spray paint.

If you want the name to read in natural terracotta, you can lift off the glue when the gold paint has completely dried .

3. Once the paint is dry, give it a coat of varnish for protection. (Always remember to wipe or handwash the pot as most spray paints, even when varnished, will not survive the dishwasher.)

4. To turn the name place into a candleholder, fill the pot with a block of dry oasis trimmed to size, cut a hole for a candle and, once you've inserted a candle of your choice, fill in the gaps with the dried moss.

Fabric sewing box

Depending on the size, fabric storage boxes can make attractive bread baskets, sewing boxes, stationery trays, or even trinket boxes. These pretty baskets are made from a simple rectangle of fabric rounded at the edges and lined in a contrasting fabric.

You will need

Cardboard box or piece of card cut
    to size
Stanley knife
Dressmaking scissors
Two pieces of contrasting fabric, as
    wide and long as the box
    flattened out, plus a ⅝in
    (1.5cm) seam allowance all
    around.
Sewing machine
Needle and thread

The easiest way of tackling this project is to use a ready made box. However, you can buy a sheet of card and make your own if you prefer.

1. Slit the box down the four corners with a Stanley knife and lay flat.

2. Using the flattened box as a template, cut out two pieces of fabric to exactly the same size, adding a ⅝in (1.5cm) seam allowance all around. Round off the corners of the fabric.

3. With right sides facing, place the fabric and lining together and machine stitch around the outside edges leaving a large enough opening along one side, to insert the roughly-folded cardboard box.

4. Snip the seam allowance at the rounded corners and trim away the excess fabric. Turn the cover right side out and press.

5. Insert the cardboard box through the opening into the fabric cover and smooth flat.

6. Neatly slipstitch the opening closed. Press flat.

7. Now re-form the box. Bring each of the four sides up so that they sit at right angles to the base. Make the fabric corners into pleats to resemble trumpet shapes (see above).

8. With a needle and thread, slipstitch the corner pleats in place. If you want the box to be completely solid, hand stitch the corners along all four sides.

Fabric photo frame and pencil pots

To use up favourite fabric scraps, collect old tins and bits of card, and with some simple cutting and sticking you can create a selection of practical and decorative gifts.

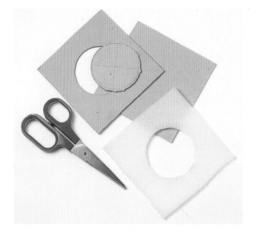

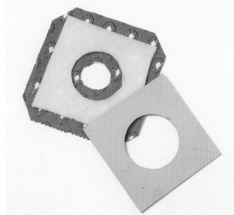

You will need:

Stanley knife or scissors
Cardboard
Pencil
Ruler
Pair of compasses
Foam wadding, ⅛in (3mm) thick
PVA glue
Small brass ring
Fabric scraps
Small tin (for the pencil pot)

1. Cut out two pieces of cardboard to the same size as your photograph.

2. On one piece of cardboard draw a diagonal line from corner to corner in order to find the centre point.

3. Place the point of the compasses in the centre of the cardboard and draw a circle to the size of your picture window. Cut out the circle with the knife.

4. Using the cardboard as a template, cut out a piece of foam, with the same central hole. Glue the foam to the cardboard.

5. Cut out two pieces of fabric to the same size as the cardboard, adding 1in (2.5cm) all around. Trim away the corners, leaving ⅛in (3mm) to spare.

6. Take the piece of fabric for the front of the frame and draw a circle (a little smaller than the first) with the compasses, as in step 2. Cut out the circle. Cut notches into the circle to enable the fabric to be pushed through the opening.

7. Next place the the foam-covered card on to the wrong side of the material. Fold over one edge of the fabric and glue to the back of the card.

8. Push through and glue the inner notched curved edge of the circle to the back of the card (see bottom left on page 21). Glue the

remaining three sides to the back of the card.

9. Take the other piece of fabric and glue to the second piece of card. Next glue the two pieces of fabric-covered card together along three sides, leaving the fourth side for the opening.

10. Sew the brass ring to the back to use as a picture hook.

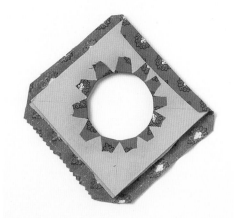

Pencil pot

1. Cut out a piece of fabric measuring the circumference of the tin by the height, adding 1in (2.5cm) all around for turnings.

2. Fold over 1in (2.5cm) turnings along the bottom edge and along one of the short back edges and glue down.

3. Glue the fabric to the tin, overlapping the neatened edge at the back. Tuck the top raw edge inside the tin and glue.

4. Instead of using glue to make turnings you could finish the edges by sticking braid around the top, back and bottom.

Finger-painted tray

Finger painting is arguably man's earliest form of painting and certainly the easiest and quickest to master. While the technique is simple and fun, the results are fresh and invigorating. Here, the fingerprints are applied on to a glazed surface which creates an interestingly textured result.

You will need:

*Tray made from Medium Density
    Fibreboard (MDF)
Household paintbrushes
Blue vinyl emulsion paint
Dusty rose pre-tinted glaze
Stippling brush
Acrylic varnish*

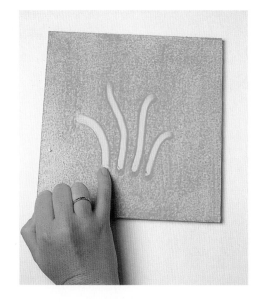

1. Make sure that the surface of the tray is clean and dry. Apply the blue emulsion basecoat with a household paintbrush.

2. When the basecoat is completely dry, apply the dusty rose pre-tinted glaze with a household paintbrush.

3. Next stipple over the wet glaze. To stipple, hold the stippling brush at a 90 degree angle to the surface and, with a quick jabbing action, dab the brush on to the surface, keeping the bristles upright. Be careful not bend the bristles.

4. While the glaze is still wet, begin your finger painting. Using your little finger, mark in the stems first and then the ribbon. For the daisy heads, use your forefinger, to give a fuller curved line. The drying time of the glaze is between 10 and 15 minutes which allows you to have another go if you make a mistake first time around. Simply paint over the fingerprints with extra glaze and start again.

5. Once the glaze is thoroughly dry, protect the surface of the tray with a coat of clear acrylic varnish.

Paper lampshades

Lampshades are notoriously prone to stains from bulbs and look grubby in no time at all. Here is an easy way of making a new shade or superimposing a new skin over an old shade using sheets of music that have been enlarged on a photocopier.

You will need:

Lampshade
Pencil
Paper
Scissors
Coin
Acetate
Black felt tip pen
Sheet music or a sheet of old-
    fashioned letters, photocopied
    and enlarged
Spray mount
PVA glue
Pegs, paper-clips or bulldog clips
Household paintbrush
Acrylic varnish

To make a completely new lampshade, back the sheet music with acetate which, unlike card, will not block the light. Be careful not to use bulbs over forty watts for safety. As an alternative to sheet music, you could buy and enlarge a piece of giftwrap with old-fashioned lettering.

1. Trace the outline of the lampshade onto a piece of paper by rolling it across the paper and adding 1in (2.5cm) to the length for overlap. Cut out the shape to make a template.

2. Lay a coin on to the curved bottom edge of the template and draw around it. Continue this process until you have a neat scalloped edge.

3. Next place the paper template on to the back of the sheet of music and cut out. If you are making a new lampshade use the template to cut out the acetate. In a well-ventilated room, spray mount the acetate and sheet music together. Leave to dry.

4. Form the shape of the lampshade and glue the sides together, holding in place using pegs, paper-clips or bulldog clips until the glue is dry.

5. If you are making a completely new paper lampshade, you will need to attach a metal frame lampshade holder to your lamp base.

6. If you are covering an old lampshade, spray mount the inside of the sheet music shade sparingly and place over the old one. Leave to dry.

7. Protect both the new and the transformed lampshade with a coat of clear acrylic varnish.

Two-hour transformations

Seen through an imaginative eye, even the blandest ingredients in a home can open up a wealth of decorative possibilities. A picture frame can be converted into a mirror vase or a candelabra; simple terracotta pots can become display items; and a plain wooden frame can be tramsformed into mahogany by painting it with vinegar.

■ Flower vase frame

■ Handpainted and glazed terracotta ware

■ Frosted window with flowerpot stencils

■ Vinegar-painted frame

■ Picture-frame candelabra

Flower vase frame

An original treatment for a standard flat frame is to give it a paint effect finish and a second function as a vase using magnetic flower holders.

You will need:

Medium Density Fibreboard (MDF) frame, approximately 12 x 14in (30 x 35cm)
Household paintbrush
Off-white vinyl silk emulsion paint
Masking tape
Pre-tinted glazes in tropical blue and mint green
Staple gun
Magnetic flower holders

Even an ornate frame can be transformed into a vase provided that it contains a flat surface within the framework wide enough to accept a large staple set at right angles. The alternative treatment shown right has metal decorative hooks fixed to the frame in the same way.

For the most professional results, a dragged paint effect requires a special dragging brush, but for small areas a household paintbrush will do equally well.

1. Paint the frame with the off-white emulsion paint. When dry, mask off the four sides of the frame along the diagonals to create mitred corners. Prepare to paint the two opposite sides of the frame first.

2. Using a household paintbrush, paint a line of tropical blue pre-tinted glaze along the outside edges. Then paint the inside with the mint green glaze. As you paint, draw the brush through the glaze in straight lines to create a dragged effect.

3. When the glaze is dry, peel off the masking tape. Then mask across the corners of the frame at a diagonal as before, applying the tape to the glaze. Paint the remaining two sides of the frame with the glaze in the same way.

4. Once the glaze is completely dry, shoot two staples next to each other into the middle of one side of the frame, about three quarters of the way down. Repeat on the other side of the frame.

Attach the magnetic flower holders to the staples. Fill the vases with water, cut stems to fit and pop in your flowers.

Handpainted and glazed terracotta ware

Terracotta ware is remarkably good value and, with a little handpainting, it can look colourful and individual. The handpainting requires no extra skill – you can fill a dresser with an afternoon's work. The pots make wonderful vases, and the shallow bowls and plates are ideal as fruit bowls.

You will need:

Household paintbrush

Off-white basecoat vinyl emulsion paint

Three pre-tinted coloured glazes in terracotta red, bright blue and bright green

Mutton cloth

Stencil brush

½in (1cm) wide one-stroke brush, (a flat rectangular-shaped brush, perfect for painting short straight lines and square blobs)

Artist's paintbrush No.12

Acrylic varnish

You can make up your own designs, but the instructions given here will help you to create the plate shown on the bottom shelf of the dresser left. One hint for making the pointed leaves, is to place the tip of the brush where you want the top of the leaf to sit and then gradually press and lift off at the opposite end. The pressure will open the brush hairs and create a soft bulge, giving the leaf or petal the right outline. If you use coloured glaze as opposed to solid colour, the results look infinitely more professional and delicate. Test out your design ideas first on a piece of tracing paper cut to the size of the plate or use a paper plate. You can fold this into eight equal sections to help you space the decorative motifs correctly.

1. Using a household paintbrush, paint the inside of the plate with off-white emulsion and leave to dry. Choose a base glaze and apply with a household paintbrush. Dab immediately with mutton cloth to obliterate the brush strokes and create a textured, cloudy effect.

2. To make the white line that encircles the plate, cover your finger with mutton cloth and run it around the inside rim. Lifting the glaze exposes the white paint below. For a coloured line, dip the stencil brush liberally into the glaze and apply in the same way, pressing and pushing it around the plate, using the rim as a guide. The excess glaze is pushed to the outside edges of the bristles, creating two lines the width of the brush. Leave to dry.

3. To make the stripes around the outside edge of the plate, use the one-stroke brush, reloading with paint when necessary. Try to keep equal spaces but do not worry too much. The rusticity of the design is often much improved by imperfections.

4. To create the intricate motifs, whether they be flowers and leaves or ribbons and dots, use the No. 12. artist's brush, working from top to bottom. It is a good idea to follow a tracing paper pattern pre-planned for this stage.

5. When dry, apply a coat of acrylic varnish. Never put the finished item in a dishwasher. Instead, clean with a damp cloth.

31

Frosted window with flowerpot stencils

Frosting a window and then decorating it with stencils is a clever way of blocking out an ugly view in a hallway or turning a dull bathroom window into a work of art.

You will need

Tape measure
Scissors
Large sheet of paper
Two-layered aricula and flowerpot
    stencil
Two-layered ivy and butterfly stencil
Spray mount adhesive
Stencil paint:
For the pot, terracotta and black
For the aricula flowers, bright pink
    and yellow
For the flower centres, bright red
    and saffron yellow
For the leaves and ivy, forest green
For the butterfly, blue, yellow
    and green
Stencil brush
Frosting varnish
2in (5cm) roller and a tray

Obviously you can vary the style of this idea. You could use a glass etch spray instead of coloured stencil paints. If you want to achieve a more traditional feel, use a Victorian-style stencil. For a classic look, use a small fleur-de-lys motif stencil, and for a less fussy effect use a modern squiggle stencil.

Before you begin make sure your window is clean, free from grease and that the glass is dry and not too cold, as any condensation will spoil the result.

1. Measure your window and cut out a piece of paper to the same dimensions so that you can plan out your design. It is advisable to stencil a trial run.

2. Once you are happy with the design, start by stencilling the flower heads and leaves, following the colours on the list opposite. Spray mount the two-layered stencil in position and and using your stencil brush complete the stencil. Leave to dry.

3. Remove the stencil. Continue to decorate the window surface. reapplying the stencil and taking care not to touch newly stencilled areas.

4. When you have finished stencilling the flower heads and leaves, stencil the three flowerpots, using terracotta paint with black paint around the edges. Leave to dry.

5. Repeat the process for the ivy and butterflies until all of the window has been decorated.

6. When you have finished stencilling the window and it is completely dry you can apply the frosting varnish. Pour a small amount of the frosting varnish into the paint tray (or an old plate). Dip the roller into the varnish, rolling off any excess onto a piece of absorbent paper or a rag. Roll the varnish over the stencilled window to create the frosted effect.

Vinegar-painted frame

Here is a quick and easy way to fake mahogany effectively. The technique uses vinegar graining, first made popular in Scandinavia. Applied to a deep terracotta base, the mahogany patina is stamped out with simple thumb and finger imprints.

You will need:

Unvarnished picture frame
Deep terracotta vinyl silk emulsion paint (matt is too absorbent)
Household paintbrush
One teaspoon of black paint pigment
Two teaspoons of raw umber paint pigment
Two teaspoons of red iron oxide paint pigment
Mixing bowl and saucer
About ½pt (280ml) of vinegar
Generous squirt of washing-up liquid
Two teaspoons sugar
Acrylic varnish

Work on a flat surface as the glaze – a mix of vinegar, washing-up liquid and paint pigments – is very runny. Don't be put off by the initial dull appearance of the graining; it only comes to life under a coat of varnish. The quantities given make enough glaze to cover a frame measuring approximately 10 x 8in (25 x 20cm). You could, however, apply this technique to any wooden surface.

1. Before you begin make sure that the frame is smooth and clean. Paint the frame with the terracotta emulsion basecoat. While this is drying, dissolve the paint pigments in cold water for five minutes, then mix together with the vinegar, washing-up liquid and sugar.

2. Apply the vinegar mixture to the frame with a paintbrush. Cover one side and a corner of the frame at a time.

3. Using the side of your hand, make a line of elongated imprints along one side of the frame, with a swift chopping action.

4. Next using the flat tip of your first finger, make a round mark to butt along the outside edge of the elongated shapes.

5. With your thumb, make a fan shape in the corner. Then repeat this process on each side of the frame.

6. Leave the frame to dry and finish by applying two coats of acrylic varnish.

Picture-frame candelabra

Create the ultimate in romantic dinner party lighting with a flower-strewn candelabra. Perfect for tables where space is at a premium, you can revamp with shiny baubles for Christmas.

You will need:

Medium Density Fibreboard (MDF) round frame about 12in (30cm) in diameter
Gold paint
Bronzing powder
Drill with ³⁄₈in (10mm) bit
Sandpaper
Small roller
White emulsion paint
Six cupboard rail sockets and screws
Screwdriver
Scissors
Natural rope
Ceiling hook
Non-drip candles (to fit rail sockets)
Real or fake ivy
Cotton wool
Staple gun

1. Paint the frame gold. You can sprinkle on some bronzing powder to make it sparkle. Leave to dry.

2. Using the ³⁄₈in (10mm) bit, drill three holes, equally spaced, around the centre of the frame. Sand any raw edges.

3. With a small roller, apply the white emulsion paint patchily. Leave to dry.

4. Screw the cupboard rail sockets to the frame, equally spaced, two between each hole.

5. Cut three pieces of thick natural rope that are long enough to hang off a ceiling-mounted hook above your dining-room table. Thread the rope upwards through the holes, and tie a knot at the end of each length of rope to hold in place.

6. Slot the candles into the cupboard rail sockets. Decorate as you please. If you are using real flowers or foliage, wrap the stems in wet cotton wool. Staple any ivy trails in position.

7. Fix the finished candelabra to the ceiling hook. Never leave the candelabra unattended.

Morning makeovers

Make the most of your morning with these decorative delights that show how you can pep up a plain cupboard and dress a window without even getting out the sewing machine. A plain table top is transformed by a woodgrained paint effect and an old cupboard is magically changed into a fake doll's-house.

- Gustavian-style cupboard

- Seersucker fan blind

- Doll's-house cupboard

- Window screen

- Gustavian-style dressing table

- Handpainted blind

- Oriental bamboo frame

- Antique-style console

Gustavian-style cupboard

You can transform a serviceable but bland wardrobe into something special by adding architectural features made from plywood cut-out shapes.

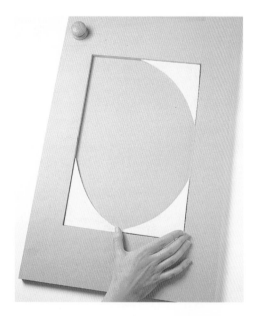

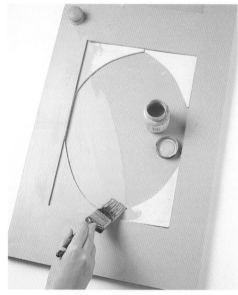

In addition to adding the cut out shapes, I turned the somewhat stocky proportions of this cupboard to advantage by increasing its height with a decorative dresser back made from carved moulding. This was screwed to a piece of plywood cut to fit the curved line of the carving.

1. Prepare your cupboard by sanding and removing any rough edges.

2. Measure the inside of the top and bottom panels of the doors and cut out paper templates to the same size. Fold the pattern for the top panel in half and in half again, and rule lines to create the diamond shapes to fit inside it. Depending on the proportions of your cupboard, you may find one diamond per door works better than two.

3. Using a plate or any circular shape as a template, draw a circle on to the paper pattern for the bottom panel.

4. Cut out the diamond and circle patterns. Using the outside pieces of the pattern, draw around these shapes on to the plywood. Carefully cut out enough shapes for both doors with a jigsaw. Sand any rough

You will need:

Tape measure
Pencil
Scissors
Paper
Ruler
Plate or circular shape
Piece of ¼in (6mm) thick plywood
Jigsaw
Wood glue
Medium-grade sandpaper
Two matching carved mouldings
Household paintbrushes
2 x 2in (5 x 5cm) timber cut to the
    width of the cupboard
Screws
Screwdriver
Grey-green emulsion paint

edges. Check that the pieces fit into the panels to create the desired shapes.

5. Apply wood glue to the cupboard fronts and plywood pieces and fix into position.

6. To make the decorative plinth, first make a paper template. Cut out a piece of paper measuring 12in (30cm) by the width of the top of the cupboard, and lay it flat on the floor. Place the decorative mouldings on to the paper at a 45° angle, joining them in the middle to create a pleasing shape for the back. Trace around the mouldings. Cut out the paper template.

7. Transfer this shape on to the plywood and carefully cut out with the jigsaw.

8. Attach the mouldings to the plywood plinth using wood glue.

9. Cut a piece of 2 x 2 in (5 x 5 cm) timber to the same width as the cupboard. Attach this to the bottom edge of the plywood with screws. Screw this in turn to the top of the cupboard.

10. Paint in grey-green emulsion paint or the colour of your choice.

Seersucker fan blind

For the non-sewing brigade, here is an opportunity to make a stylish fan-shaped blind in frothy cream seersucker with hardly any sewing involved.

You will need:

Fabric to cover the width and length of the window (plus extra fabric added to the width to allow for the pleat, and hem allowances, see step 1)
Needle and thread
Iron-on tape
Eyelet kit with eyelets
Blind cord
½in (1cm) square wooden batten the same width as your window
Two screw eyes
Cleat hook
Staple gun
Tassel
Brackets with screws

1. Measure the width and depth of your window, adding 14in (35cm) to the width (12in (30cm) for the pleat and 1in (2.5cm) for side hems), and 2in (5cm) to the length for top and bottom hems. Cut out the fabric to this size. Depending on the width of your window, you may need to sew fabric widths together.

2. Turn over double ½in (1cm) hems at the top, bottom and sides and sew or secure with iron-on tape.

3. Next, make a 3in (7.5cm) deep pleat in the middle of the blind to take up the extra 12in (30cm).

Secure in place with a line of stitching (see illustration right).

4. Beginning at the bottom of the pleat in the middle and following the instructions on the eyelet kit, secure the first eyelet. Then run a line of eyelets in pairs about 1½in (4cm) apart, leaving 8in (20cm) between the pairs along the middle of the blind.

5. Thread and knot the blind cord to the bottom eyelet and running the cord along the wrong side of the fabric, thread between the eyelet pairs (see detail, below right).

6. Screw the brackets to the wooden batten. Fix the screw eyes to the batten, one in the middle and the other to one end. And then screw a cleat hook halfway up the side of the window frame.

7. Attach the blind to the batten, using the staple gun. Thread the blind cord through the two screw eyes (the middle one first). Fix the tassel to the central cord at the bottom edge.

8. Fix the batten in position, securing it inside or outside the reveal. To raise the blind pull the cord and wind in a figure of eight around the cleat hook.

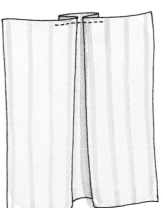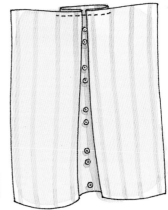

Doll's-house cupboard

Here is an imaginative way of giving old cupboard doors in a child's room a new lease of life using paint and stencils. Designed for the dedicated parent who can use a fretsaw the window and the front door shape can be cut out and screwed on to hinges.

You will need

Pencil
Brown paper
Measuring tape
Scissors
Screwdriver
White spirit
Straight edge
Masking tape
Household paintbrushes
Acrylic colours in off-white, yellow,
    blue, grey and black
Stencil brushes
Oil stencil crayons in black, brown,
    blue, green and brick red
Stencil set that includes balustrading,
    column capitals, windows, bay
    trees and a front door
Piece of paper or card
Acrylic varnish
Spray mount

Test out your design first on a piece of brown paper cut to the same size as the cupboard doors, and draw in the different elements of the façade. Also, unhinge the cupboard doors so that you have a flat surface to work on. Use oil stencil crayons which do not smudge, then if you make a mistake you can remove it with white spirit and start again. For really convincing results and a three-dimensional effect, keep the middle parts of a stencil lightest and shade heaviest around the outside. Shading the roof line and columns is particularly important. For an overall variety of texture and colour, you can overlap stencil colours but remember to use a separate brush for each colour.

1. With a pencil and straight edge, mark lines for the columns, roof line, sloping pediment and, if there is room, a grass verge. Mask off these elements. Use three parallel lines of masking tape for the sloping roof.

2. Paint the sky blue and the body of the building in pale yellow. When dry, remask the lines alongside the columns. Paint in grey at the outside edges and blue in the middle.

3. Pull off the middle piece of masking tape along the roof line and paint in grey. Remask the roof line to paint the top of the roof in a darker shade of grey (add black to your existing grey). Paint the line below in dark

yellow. Remask the roof line again and shade below using a stencil brush lightly dipped in grey acrylic paint.

4. To use stencil crayons, first apply the stick in a circular motion, drawing a small round circle on a piece of ordinary paper or card. Then lift off the colour by pushing the stencil brush on to the patch of colour using the same circular motion. Once the brush is loaded, apply to the stencil using the same circular scrubbing action.

5. Stencil the balustrading and column capitals with the black and brown crayons. Apply masking tape to the bottom of the line of balustrading and shade below with a stencil brush. Mask the columns in the same way, shading on the right side only so that they appear to stand proud of the walls.

6. Stencil the windows, shading the body in grey and the frames in blue. Finally, stencil the front door and bay tree.

7. Apply at least two or three coats of acrylic varnish to protect the finished doors. When dry, screw the doors back on to the cupboard.

Window screen

For the many windows in urban areas where clear sky is enjoyed above eye level but brick walls below are overlooked, a half-height screen covered in a pretty fabric is great compensation for the lack of colour outside.

You will need:

Screwdriver

A flat screen which blocks out about two-thirds of the window

Flowerpot fabric to cover the front panels (or fabric of your choice)

Tailor's chalk

Dressmaker's scissors

Medium-weight Terylene wadding to cover back and front panels

Checked fabric to cover back panels (or fabric of your choice)

Staple gun

Fabric glue

Braid to surround the perimeter of the panels

An additional idea to enhance your sky view is to place plants on a shelf spanning the window.

Mine are in blue and white pots that match those printed on the fabric covering the screen.

1. Unscrew the screen panels. Lay one panel on to the facing (flowerpot) fabric and draw around the shape with tailor's chalk. Cut out the panel adding 4in (10cm) all around for turnings.

2. Using this panel as a template, cut out as many fabric panels as required for the front and back of the screen and then cut out the wadding pieces to the same size.

3. Lay the wadding on to the front of the first screen panel and place the flower pot fabric on top. Stretch and wrap it around

the screen edges, and staple to the back of the screen. Secure the second staple to the opposite side of the panel. Shoot a staple at the top and bottom to keep the fabric smooth.

4. Continue stapling until the top cover is secure, leaving 1in (2.5cm) gaps between staples. For neat corners, fold the fabric at a 45° angle and line up the fold with the corner of the frame. Repeat this process to cover all four panels.

5. Turn the panels over and place the checked fabric on top. Fold in the raw edges just below the screen edge. Staple the fabric to the screen panels as before.

6. To cover the staples, glue on strips of braid. Replace the hinges using the original screw holes.

Gustavian-style dressing table

It can take many years for paintwork to achieve an attractive, mellowed look, but there are short cuts to help reproduce the effects of time. Of all the ways to achieve instant ageing for inexpensive furniture, none is as easy and effective as layered painting, where pre-tinted glazes are used over a base colour to build up a richly varied patina.

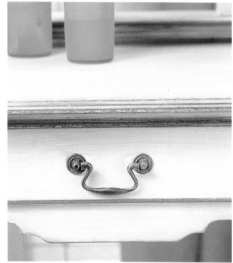

You will need:

Terracotta emulsion paint
2in (5cm) paintbrush
*Medium Density Fibreboard (MDF)
     writing table in an antique style*
Masking tape
Household candle
Gold stencil paint
Ivory white vinyl silk emulsion paint
*Apple-green colourwash (a pretinted
     glaze)*
Fine-grade sandpaper
Decorator's acrylic varnishing wax

The elegant appeal of 18th-century Swedish furniture – known as Gustavian – has never been greater. Real antiques are expensive and scarce but here is an easy colour-layered recipe in off-white and gold to recreate the pale, graceful Gustavian look.

1. Apply a coat of terracotta emulsion paint to the dressing table. Leave to dry.

2. When dry, mask off the legs and edges to be painted in gold and, using an ordinary household candle, rub wax over the outer edges, drawer edges and legs. Paint a thin coat of gold stencil paint on top.

3. Remove the tape and reapply to mask off the table top, front, back and sides. Paint these areas with a thin coat of ivory white emulsion paint. Leave to dry. Then, with fine sandpaper, rub away some of the white to reveal patches of the terracotta emulsion basecoat.

4. Paint over the surface again, this time with a layer of apple-green colourwash. When dry, seal with varnishing wax.

5. The dressing table mirror was painted in the same colours and in the same sequence, but with slightly more vigorous use of the sandpaper to achieve a stronger distressed effect. The stool was painted in ivory white emulsion paint first and then given a top coat of the apple green colourwash.

Handpainted blind

If you like shutters, but are not too confident working with wood, a blind, made from black out material and hung from a portier rod, is a good alternative. You can paint your favourite images directly on to the blind with fabric paint or pens.

You will need

Scissors

A piece of stiff black-out material cut to the size of your window, plus 4in (10cm) for the casing

Sewing machine

Ruler and pencil

Fabric paint pens in blue, green, grey, and yellow or thick felt tip pens

Tracing paper

Sticky tape (to hold tracing and carbon paper in place)

Carbon paper

A portier rod

Hacksaw

Screws and screwdriver

The advantage of using stiff black-out material is that the material does not fray and there is very little sewing involved.

A tip for using fabric paint pens is to apply them lightly to prevent them running.

For the smoothest texture, felt-tips should be drawn in one direction only across each shape. It's best to let each colour dry first before you begin working with another.

1. Cut out the black-out material to the size of your window adding 4in (10cm) to the length for the casing.

2. To make the casing fold over a 4in (10cm) hem to the wrong side along the top edge and machine stitch in place.

3. Draw a fake window frame on the fabric using a ruler and thin black felt-tip pen.

4. Trace, photocopy and enlarge your chosen images and transfer them to the blind using carbon paper (see above). Alternatively you can copy the clouds, bird and flower design shown here.

5. Paint the images with fabric paint or thick felt tip pens. Leave to dry.

6. Cut the portier rod to size with the hacksaw. Screw to the top corner of the window reveal and slot the blind in place.

Oriental bamboo frame

As a contrast to using curtains or wall hangings to fill blank wall space behind a bed, simple bamboo screens make a soothingly simple visual statement and inject a measure of Japanese tranquillity into the bedroom. Ideal for a minilmalist style, the idea can be prettied up or pared down according to fabric choice.

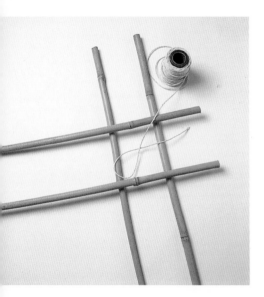 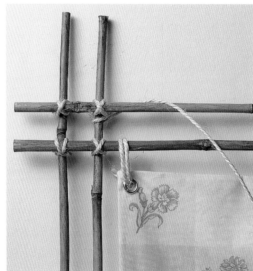 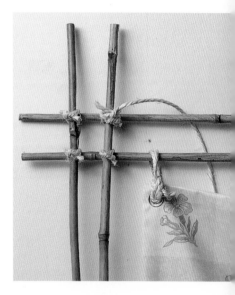

You will need:

Sewing thread, scissors and pins
Fabric
Sewing machine
Eyelet kit with eyelets
Bamboo canes
Hacksaw
Wood glue
String
Picture hooks

The size and shape of these panels can be altered to suit the dimension of the wall space you want to fill but on the whole two or three matching panels in a row or staggered as shown here,

make a more sophisticated graphic statement than one bamboo frame on its own.

1. Decide on the size and number of panels that you want to make. Cut out two pieces of fabric for each panel, adding ½in (1cm) all around for seam allowances.

2. For each panel of the screen, place the two pieces of fabric right sides facing and machine stitch around all four sides, leaving a small 6in (15cm) gap along one side. Turn the fabric right side out and then press.

3. Following the instructions in the eyelet kit, position an eyelet in each of the four corners of the fabric panel.

4. Cut four pieces of bamboo to the same length as the fabric panel plus 20in (51cm), and four pieces to the same width of the panel plus 12in (30cm).

5. Lay the bamboo out flat on the floor, overlapping the ends to form a noughts and crosses effect. To stop the bamboo from slipping, dab some wood glue between the sticks at the points to be tied with string.

6. Secure the bamboo pieces with string wound around the crossing points. You can do this any way you choose as long as the end result is neat. Cut off any loose ends.

7. Thread a piece of string to make a double loop through each of the four eyelets in the fabric panels and tie on to the top and bottom of the frame.

8. Tie string to the top of the two corners of each panel and hang from a picture hook.

Antique-style console

This plain and uninteresting Medium Density Fibreboard (MDF) table has been painted in layers of glaze and then limed and stencilled to transform it into a delicate antique-style console table.

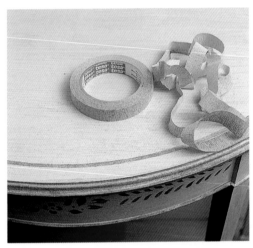

You will need:

Household paintbrush
Mint green vinyl silk emulsion paint
Ivory white vinyl silk emulsion paint
Pre-tinted blue glaze
Flexible masking tape
Blue stencil stick
Paper
Stencil brush
Leaf and half crescent stencil
Sandpaper
Acrylic varnishing wax
Soft cloth

1. Apply a mint green basecoat and leave to dry.

2. Next apply a watered-down layer of ivory white emulsion paint. The proportions should be about fifty-fifty.

3. Apply a coat of pre-tinted blue glaze. You can also mix your own using scumble and cobalt blue acrylic paint.

4. When thoroughly dry (leave overnight if possible), mask two curved parallel lines around the top edge of the table using the flexible masking tape, leaving a narrow ½in (1cm) gap between the lines. Rub the blue stencil stick on to a piece of paper and lift off the pigment with a stencil brush. With a rotary action, rub the pigment on to the exposed area to create the blue line.

5. Apply the leaf and half crescent stencil using the blue stencil stick. After 24 hours drying time, rub gently with sandpaper to exaggerate the aged look.

6. Apply a layer of polyvine acrylic varnishing wax using a soft cloth.

TIPS FOR ANTIQUING

1. When choosing colours, remember that when people first started decorating furniture, the range of colours was limited. Earth pigments, which make yellow ochre, muddy greens and brown reds were readilyx available. To dull modern colours, finish with a coat of furniture wax or shoe polish.

2. If possible, use a no-loss paint brush. When using an old brush, if hairs get stuck in the glaze, remove them before it dries.

3. Instead of a paintbrush, experiment with a small 2in (5cm) roller which produces a patchy effect.

4. To expose more of the base colour in the right place, use fine sanding paper around areas that you would expect to receive the most wear and tear.

5. For painting straight lines around drawers and table tops, use a masking tape which is low tack and less likely to remove paintwork when pulled away.

Evening Escapades

Projects to absorb one after an exhausting day's work need to be relaxing and not too challeging. As one person's idea of what constitutes a fun creative evening is not another's, here are a varied selection of inventive decorative solutions to choose from.

- Woodgrained and stencilled table top

- Goblet-headed curtains

- Trompe l'oeil kitchen dresser

- Clover leaf shutters

- Decoupage firescreen

- Fake china cupboard with chicken wire

- Stencilled pine chair

- Coffee table stool

Woodgrained and stencilled table top

A piece of melamine is transformed into a decorative wooden table top by giving it an imitation grain created with pre-tinted glazes and a woodgrainer. For a garden table style, the stencilled border and corners are applied with a sponge in two colours.

You will need:

Medium-grade sandpaper
Soft cloth
Acrylic convertor or a good-quality tile or plastic primer
Pre-tinted pine green glaze
Pre-tinted pale grey glaze
Household paintbrushes
Wide decorator's brush
Large loose-patterned woodgrainer
Corner and border stencil
Spray mount
Natural sponge
Khaki green and dark grey stencil paint
Water- and heat-resistant varnish

1. Sand down the melamine surface with the sandpaper to prepare it for painting. Rub clean then apply an acrylic convertor or a similar suitable primer.

2. When thoroughly dry (it can take 24 hours) apply the two shades of pre-tinted glaze with an ordinary household brush in separate, random patches. Be careful not to mix the colours.

3. While the glazes are still wet, brush in a lengthwise direction with a wide decorator's brush. Once the surface is evenly covered, rebrush in a straight line down the length of the surface, pushing down hard, to create three separate lines about 8in (20cm) apart that look like grooves between planks of wood.

4. Run the woodgrainer down the "planks" in the same direction using a gentle rocking action. Pull the grainer in one continuous flow. As most glazes take around 10–15 minutes to dry, you will have time to re-do any mistakes.

5. When dry, attach the corner and border stencil with spray mount. Using a natural sponge, apply the stencil paint in khaki green and then dark grey to achieve a rough mottled effect.

6. When dry, apply three coats of water- and heat-resistant varnish.

Goblet-headed curtains

For a contemporary rendering of an old favourite, goblet-headed curtains can be quickly made using an eyelet kit, with only a minimum of simple sewing involved. Obviously a bonus for non-sewers, these curtains look surprisingly professional.

You will need:

Tape measure and scissors
Fabric to fit your window (see text)
Sewing machine
Needle, thread and pins
*5in (13cm) wide stiffened inter-
lining, the width of your curtain
less the width of the side hem*
Eyelet kit (six eyelets per goblet)
Small brass rings (one per pleat)

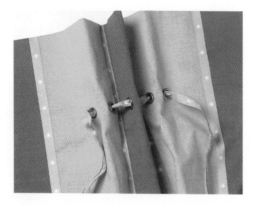

Traditionally goblet-headed curtains are handsewn. I've devised a method which requires only a modicum of sewing. Choosing a striped fabric makes the job much easier. For example, the narrowest stripe in this fabric is a perfect width for the ties which thread through the eyelets and hold the goblets in place.

1. Measure the length of your window and add 8in (20cm) for the heading and 6in (15cm) for the hem to your fabric length.

2. Work out how many widths you will need for each curtain by measuring your curtain pole. Each pleat takes up 10in (25cm) in the width of the curtain, and between each pleat there is a gap of 9in (22cm). Obviously you can alter these measurements to suit the dimensions of your windows.

3. Cut the fabric to length and make up the curtains, stitching right sides together lengthwise to create the desired curtain width.

4. Pin, tack and seam all the raw edges and turn up the hem line. Press all hems.

5. Make a 1in (2.5cm) fold along the top of each curtain and then a 5in (13cm) fold and press.

6. Cut a strip of stiffened interlining to the same width of the curtain and place within the fold. Tack in place.

7. Following the instructions on the eyelet kit, work out the positions for the row of eyelets which should sit just below interlining. Start the first pleat at the side edge of the fabric. To make one pleat you need a row

of six equally spaced eyelets with 1in (2.5cm) gaps between them. Leave equal spaces between the beginning and end of each pleat.

8. Make up narrow ribbons of fabric, ½in (1cm) wide by 22in (56cm) long, allowing one for each pleat. Thread through the row of six eyelets and pull tight. Knot with a simple bow.

9. Sew a small brass ring to the back of each tie and attach to the rings on the curtain pole.

ALTERATIVE IDEAS

Two alternative ways to make curtain headings with eyelets are to thread coloured piping to make rings or just slip on decorative hooks for fixed curtains with tie-backs.

Trompe l'oeil kitchen dresser

The china cupboard you have always wanted but have not been able to afford can be stencilled on to a kitchen wall at the fraction of the price of the real thing. Add a few pieces of china to create the ultimate double bluff.

HOMEMADE STENCIL

You will need:

Your chosen design
Piece of glass
Acetate
Masking tape or spray mount
Hot pen

Architraves, shaped moulding and even drawers are easy to represent with the help of masking tape and stencil crayons.

You can buy ready-made stencils for the fake crockery or make your own, as shown here.

1. It is a good idea to photograph the mugs or trace the plates that you want to stencil and then enlarge the images on a photocopier. The enlarging process should separate the shapes and create the necessary bridges required to make a stencil. Use the originals as sources of inspiration and feel free to simplify the design. You

may find it helpful to add your own amendments – for instance, creating a wreath of leaves inside the outer rim of a plate stencil will add definition.

2. Once you are satisfied with your finished design, carefully place a piece of glass below it and secure a piece of acetate the same size on top using masking tape or spray mount.

3. Trace around the lines of your design on to the acetate with a

hot pen. To add dimension and depth, make a layered stencil. For instance, to add an outer rim to the plate, place a second sheet of acetate over the photocopied plate design and draw a narrow outer edge to frame the lowest circle of the plate, remembering to include at least six tiny "bridges" equally spaced around the circumference. These will hold the stencil together.

TROMPE L'OEIL DRESSER

You will need:

Measuring tape and straight edge
Pencil and ruler
Plumb line
Masking tape
Sheets of plain paper
Scissors
Stencil sticks in brown, black and
    assorted colours for the crockery
Stencil brushes

Spray mount
Stencils for jugs, plates, cups,
    tureen and shelf brackets
Acrylic varnish
Household paintbrushes
Drill, wall plugs, plate hangers
    and cuphooks

1. Mark out the size and position of the dresser top on your wall and the shelves, shelf brackets and surrounding framework.

Draw lines in pencil to mark their positions on the wall using the ruler and plumb line.

2. Use masking tape to define the top line of the dresser. Design and cut a shape for the top moulded corner edge or mask off a simple curve.

3. Mask the shelves, leaving a 1in (2.5cm) gap between the two rows of tape.

4. Stencil sticks are not intended to be used as a normal crayon. To use them, rub the colour on to a piece of paper first and then, with a circular motion, pick up the crayon pigment by rubbing the stencil brush bristles on to the paper. Using a mixture of brown and black stencil crayon, fill in the spaces between the masking tape to create shelves and a 2in (5cm) wide dresser top with very slightly curved ends.

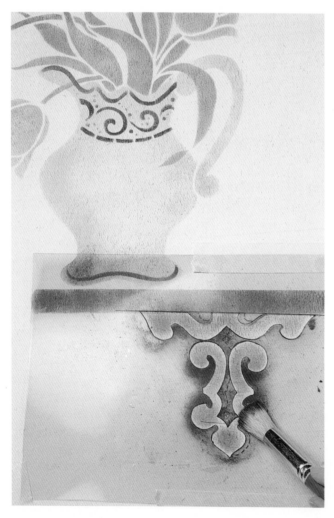

Reposition the masking tape to create a second 1in (2.5cm) wide line of false shelving, leaving a gap of about 18 in (46cm) in between. Using spray mount, position and stencil a two-layered shelf bracket below the shelves.

5. Decide on the position of the fake china and where you want to hang the real mugs and plates.

Lightly cover the back of each stencil in spray mount and press on to the wall. Using the stencils as a palette, rub the stencil stick on to the blank area keeping well away from the cut-out sections.

6. Pick up a colour on the stencil brush as before and use a circular motion to transfer the colour to the wall. Shade the stencil darker around the edges

to create a three-dimensional effect. Do not worry about overlapping colours as this serves to add interest and texture. It is worth overlapping yellow and orange in the tulips and introducing extra colour to the leaves. For really professional results, shade the outside edge of each outline shape after you have peeled away the stencil. This will make the shapes stand out.

7. When you have completed the stencilling, leave the wall to dry for 48 hours. To protect the stencils, apply a coat of clear varnish. Test a tiny section first to make sure the colour is dry.

8. Drill holes for cuphooks and plate hangers and position the real china in place.

Clover leaf shutters

For deeply set windows where curtains and blinds won't fit or threaten to block out too much light, shutters are an excellent alternative. When open, they allow in maximum sunlight and closed, they can make the room look cheerful and cosy. I've decorated these Medium Density Fibreboard (MDF) shutters with a cut-out clover leaf motif, which involves using a special drill head but not above-average carpentry skills.

You will need:

Measuring tape
Medium Density Fibreboard (MDF)
    ½in (1cm) thick, sold in 8ft
    (2.6m) by 4ft (1.2m) sheets
Hacksaw
Glasspaper or fine sandpaper
Pair of compasses and pencil
A holesaw with 2in (5cm) diameter
    circular saw bit and a
    standard drill bit and a ⅛in
    (2mm) drill bit
Piano hinges 36in (91cm) in length
    with countersunk screws to fit
Glue in a mastic gun
Screwdriver
Vinyl silk emulsion paint
Household paintbrush
Magnetic catches (optional)

If you want to let in more light when the shutters are closed, drill extra motifs into them. A multitude of stars of varying sizes works well, and you could also try mixing them with crescent moons.

1. To make the shutters, measure the window recess and cut the MDF to size with the hacksaw (or have it pre-cut at a timber merchants).

2. Using the glasspaper, smooth the rough edges left by the saw.

3. To cut out the clover shape, draw four overlapping 2in (5cm) diameter circles using the pair of compasses and pencil,

positioning them in the centre of each shutter width, about 8in (20cm) from the top.

4. With an ordinary drill bit, drill a hole in the middle of each pencilled circle to use as a guide for the holesaw.

5. With the holesaw and circular saw bit, cut out the circles to form the clover shape. Smooth the rough edges with glasspaper.

6. Using the hacksaw, cut the piano hinges to the same length as the long side of the shutters.

7. Decide which way the hinges will fit on the shutters so they open fully. Open the hinge on

each shutter and place one side to rest against the face of the MDF. Glue in place along the edge of the shutter and wipe off any excess glue.

8. To screw the hinges in place, drill pilot holes for each screw using a ⅛in (2mm) drill bit, which will prevent the MDF from splitting as the screws are driven in. Put a screw in each hole and make sure the head of the screw sits below the surface of the hinge.

9. Paint the shutters with two coats of emulsion and, when dry, screw the free side of the piano hinge to the window reveal. Fix the magnetic catches, if using.

Decoupage firescreen

*Decoupage is one of the easiest ways to decorate an object –
it simply involves sticking cut-out images on to a flat surface.
To guarantee success, images should come from the same source –
from a piece of wallpaper or a book of flower prints, perhaps. This
firescreen was given a sponged paint effect and then decorated
with images from a single piece of quality wrapping paper.*

A reliable way to pre-plan your design is to apply spray mount to the back of your cut-outs and stick them to the surface. Because spray mount is such a light adhesive, it allows you to re-jig the pieces until you achieve the desired results. If you do use cut-outs from a variety of sources, try to link them by colour or choose images in the same genre – a variety of seed packets, old cards or Victorian scraps, for instance.

1. For the sponged paint effect, apply two coats of off-white vinyl silk emulsion to the firescreen, allowing each coat to dry before applying the next.

2. Pour the different glazes into three separate plates and dip the natural sponge into the pale yellow first. Dab the sponge on to a piece of kitchen paper and then lightly dab over the firescreen, changing the angle of your wrist to vary the imprints.

3. Apply the ochre glaze in the same way. Finally, apply the terracotta very sparingly. The

glazes can be applied immediately on top of each other. You don't need to leave them to dry in between applications.

4. Cut out the chosen images accurately and position them in place with spray mount. Once you are happy with the overall design, apply the paper glue to the back of each cut-out.

5. With the soft cloth or kitchen paper, press each piece in place carefully (be sure to smooth away any air bubbles). Add extra glue at any point where the paper curls up at the edges.

6. Leave the work to dry overnight and then apply five to six thin coats of acrylic varnish. The aim is to apply enough varnish so that the paper appears to be embedded into the surface rather than just stuck on.

You will need:

Off-white vinyl silk emulsion
Household paintbrushes
Unpainted Medium Density

Fibreboard (MDF)
    firescreen
Three different glazes in pale
    yellow, ochre and
    terracotta
Three cardboard plates or paint
    containers
Natural sponge
Kitchen paper
Sharp scissors
Sheet of wrapping paper or
    your chosen images
Spray mount
Paper glue
Soft cloth
Acrylic varnish

Fake china cupboard with chicken wire

An ingenious way of concealing a rubbish swingbin in a kitchen is to place it in a converted cupboard with a lift-up top. Add a stencilled trompe l'oeil "china cupboard" effect to the front for complete decorative deception.

You will need:

Cupboard with hinged lift-up top,
    large enough to fit your
    swingbin inside
Household paintbrushes
Custard-yellow vinyl silk emulsion
Screwdriver
Pencil
Low-tack masking tape
Pre-tinted grey glaze
Black acrylic paint
Spray mount
Three-layered plate stencil
Two-layered jug stencil
Dark blue acrylic paint
Stencil brushes
Small paint roller
White vinyl silk emulsion
Oil-based blue stencil crayon
Paper
Water-based bright blue stencil
    paint
Chicken wire
Staple gun
½in (1cm) wide wooden moulding
Handsaw and mitre block
Tacks and tack hammer
Blue and white door knob

The success of this project relies hugely upon achieving a realistic three-dimensional effect. It is vital to be consistent about the angle at which the light is seen to fall on each object and the shadow cast. This demands sustained concentration while you work, but no outstanding artistic skills.

1. Paint the cupboard using the yellow emulsion (or the colour of your choice). Leave to dry.

2. As it is easier to work on a flat surface, unscrew the door hinges to remove the doors. Within the inset door panel, pencil in the positions for four shelf lines of masking tape. The first one

should be about one third from the top, the second about halfway down, the third should match the first gap and the fourth should mask the bottom gap where the inset door panel meets the door frame.

3. With the pre-tinted grey glaze, paint the two masked-off

strips to make your pretend shelves. As you paint the strips, drag the brush horizontally.

4. When dry, reposition the masking tape to protect the "shelves" and to enable you to paint the "back" of the cupboard. Darken the grey glaze with black acrylic paint and work the paint by dragging the brush downwards at right angles to the fake shelves. Leave to dry.

5. Spray mount the stencil plate and jug outline in place. Using dark blue acrylic paint, paint in the inside of the shapes with a paintbrush for quick coverage. Use a fine stencil brush for the outside edges.

6. With the same outline shape, roller over the blue patchily with white emulsion. This makes the surface look like hand-fired china. Leave to dry.

7. Next rub some dark blue oil-based stencil crayon on to a piece of paper and, using the same outline for the plate and jug stencil, give the shapes a three-dimensional effect by shading the outside edge of the plate. Decide which side the light source is positioned and concentrate the shading to one side.

8. Using the second stencil layer of the plate, stencil with the same blue crayon to create a rim shape shadow to the plate.

9. Finally, stencil stipple a bright blue paint on to the third layer of the plate stencil, and the second layer of the jug stencil giving the crockery a decorative pattern. Shade the back of the jug and plate around the outlines (along the shade side only) using a stencil brush dipped in the pre-tinted grey glaze mixed with the black used previously.

10. Saw the chicken wire to fit into the panel. Staple in place.

11. Cut the mouldings to fit the panels using a small handsaw. Using a mitre block, cut the moulding at a 45° angle. Tack in place with a tack hammer as an ordinary hammer is likely to split

the wood. These wooden mouldings should overlap and conceal the raw edges of the chicken wire.

12. Screw back the cupboard door and attach the door knob.

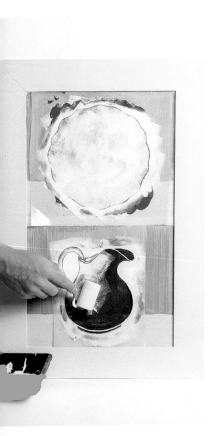

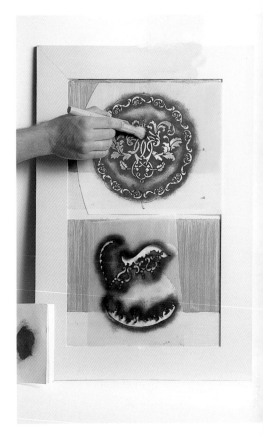

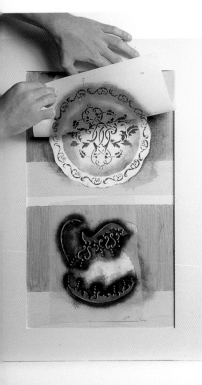

Stencilled pine chair

Combine stencilling with simple handpainting and ageing techniques to transform a new pine chair into a delightful handcrafted antique.

You will need:

Off-white, yellow ochre and blue-grey emulsion
2in (5cm) wide paintbrushes
½in (1cm) wide masking or low-tack tape
½in (1cm) wide flexible tape
Medium-size artist's brush
Scissors, paper and pencil
Leaf and berry stencils
Spray mount
Stencil paint in green, red and dark grey
Stencil brushes
Acrylic varnish
Boot polish or antiquing wax
Soft cloth
Clear furniture wax

1. Paint the chair in an off-white emulsion and leave to dry.

2. Position the masking tape to create the off-white stripes around the seat, up the two vertical sides of the frame and to frame the seat back. Paint the unmasked areas in blue and yellow ochre (see main picture). Paint the legs blue and the cross bar of the seat in yellow. Obviously you can adapt colours to suit your own artistic inclination but it is a good idea to keep some white showing as it will lift and brighten the overall effect and set off the handpainted decoration.

3. Using the flexible tape, mask a curve on the top of the chair back. Paint in a narrow blue line and when dry, remask to paint the adjoining strip using the yellow ochre.

4. Before stencilling the chair back, work out a design that you like and that fills the area well. If in doubt, cut out a piece of paper to the same size as the back and experiment with colours.

5. Transfer your composition to the chair with stencils, secured with spray mount, using green for the leaves and crimson red for the berries.

6. Once dry, join the leaves to the stems obliterating any tell-tale stencil "bridges" with an artist's brush. Decide which way the light is to fall and then high-light the leaves with a pale off-white line mixed with a tiny bit of green. Paint each line in one movement, starting lightly at the top tip of the leaf, and then pressing down harder to make a wider line in the middle. Then release the pressure to make it fade out at the bottom.

7. Make up a second darker green and paint the opposite side of the leaf with darker shading. If the contrast seems too dynamic, blend the two lines, shading them in the middle of the leaf.

8. Dip the paintbrush into the off-white emulsion and make a tiny dot on each berry to act as a highlight. Again, be consistent with your decision on light direction. Each berry needs to be lit in roughly the same spot. Be careful not to overpaint your work and end up with a muddy picture with its freshness and definition impaired.

9. When thoroughly dry, apply a protective coat of acrylic varnish.

10. To give an antique effect, rub on boot polish or antiquing wax in patches with a cloth. Rub well into the surface and leave to dry. Add a final coat of clear furniture wax and polish with a soft cloth.

Coffee table stool

Converting a melamine table into a classy upholstered stool is easier than you might think. The essential ingredients are fabric, wadding and a staple gun. For the best result, use good-quality fabric with a sumptuous fringe to match, and disguise the melamine under fake mahogany legs.

MAHOGANY GRAINING

You will need:

Old melamine coffee table
Medium-grade sandpaper
Soft cloth
PVA glue and brush
Terracotta vinyl silk emulsion paint
Household paintbrush
Artist's acrylic colours in burnt
    umber, raw sienna and Mars
    black
Scumble glaze
Woodgrainer
Softening brush
Matt acrylic varnish

1. Sand the table legs and rub clean. Then apply a coat of PVA glue and leave to dry thoroughly.

2. Apply two coats of the terracotta emulsion.

3. Make up a glaze, using one part burnt umber and one part raw sienna with a bead-size spot of Mars black to three parts scumble glaze.

4. Carefully apply the glaze to the table legs with a household paintbrush, working in a lengthwise direction only.

5. Pull the woodgrainer through the glaze, rocking it gently to create a loose elongated heart-grained pattern. This may take a bit of practice but remember that you can wipe it smooth and start again if you need to since the glaze will remain wet for at least five minutes.

6. Soften the effect with the softening brush by just lightly stroking the surface in the direction of the painted grain.

7. When the glaze is dry, apply a coat of acrylic varnish to finish.

UPHOLSTERED SEAT

You will need:

Tape measure and scissors
Thick Terylene wadding
2in (5cm) wide heavy duty
    parcel tape
Foam pillow
Staple gun
Upholstery fabric to cover the
    stool (see text)
Fabric glue
Upholstery fringe

1. Measure the top of the stool, adding 6in (15cm) all round. Cut the Terylene wadding to this size. For the edges, make up four sausage-roll shapes of wadding.

Cut two to the same width as the stool and 15in (38cm) long, and two to the length of the stool minus 7in (18cm). Roll each piece tightly to make a sausage shape and bind with tape.

2. Centre the foam pillow in the middle of the stool, and fit the rolls of wadding around the side edges. Tape these in place. Lay a flat piece of wadding over them and staple in place.

3. Cut the upholstery fabric to fit over the stool, allowing for a 1in (2.5cm) fold to hide the raw edges. Fix in place with a row of staples: start with one at the centre of each side and leave the corners until last. Fold the side edges in to make two neat folds.

4. Glue the upholstery fringe over the line of staples.

Same-day Sensations

With a clear day ahead of you, why not master a whole new paint effect, such as faux marquetry, malachite, marble or inlaid granite? Or try a new craft, such as mosiac or transform furniture?

- Faux inlaid granite table top

- Fake trellis doors

- Faux marquetry table top

- Office chair transformation

- Mosaic table top

- Sofa divan transformation

- Fake inlaid marble

- Tented shelving

- Faux malachite with gold leaf

- Marbled table top with malachite inlay

Faux inlaid granite table top

This stunning transformation from chipboard to weathered inlaid granite is achieved with a simple star design and mellow, classy colours. Set on a low base, it makes a smart and useful coffee table.

You will need:

Off-white vinyl silk emulsion paint
Household paintbrushes
Square chipboard table top
Coloured glazes in mustard, grey-green, dark blue green, forest green and dark grey
Mutton cloth
½in (1cm) wide low-tack masking tape
Cotton cloth
Stippling brush
Piece of brown paper cut to the size of the table top
Pencil and straight edge
Three templates made from circular objects of different diameters, such as a dinner plate, large bowl and small circular table top
String (optional)
Steel rule and Stanley knife
Spray mount
Stencil brush
Old toothbrush
Scrap paper
Bronze or gold powder
Acrylic varnish

As with all projects, this design could be coloured in any number of ways. I chose to work with greens, but autumnal colours or shades of purple and blue could look stunning. A monochrome scheme would be quite easy to match with your existing china.

1. Apply two coats of off-white vinyl silk emulsion paint to the table top. Allow each coat to dry before applying the next one.

2. Paint the mustard glaze on top of the dried emulsion with an ordinary paintbrush, working it in all directions and spreading it out very thinly. Go over the surface again with the tip of the brush to make it as smooth and even as possible and to obliterate the brushstrokes as far as possible. Fold the mutton cloth into a smooth pad and dab it over the surface. If necessary, refold the pad to a clean part as the glaze

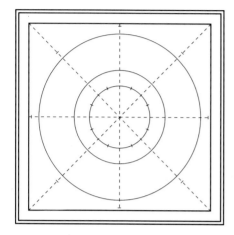

DIAGRAM 1

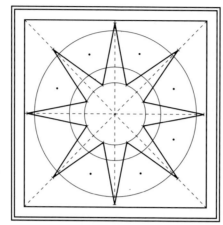

DIAGRAM 2

DIAGRAM 3

accumulates. The overall effect should be soft and even. Leave to dry thoroughly.

3. With two lines of ½in (1cm) wide masking tape, mask off a 2in (5cm) wide band, ½in (1cm) in from the outside edge. Cover the surface in between with the grey-green glaze. To ensure that the masking tape does not take off the first glaze, use a low-tack tape and before applying it, lift off more of the glue from the tape by applying it to a piece of cotton cloth (a T-shirt or sheet is ideal). Apply the green glaze with an ordinary brush in all directions to spread it evenly. Then, as before, go over the surface with the tip of the brush to obliterate the brush strokes as far as possible. Using a large stippling brush, stab the surface with a steady strong motion, hitting the surface directly at a 90° angle. Repeat the action to overlap the previous area. The finished effect should be evenly and finely

speckled. Allow to dry and then repeat the process using the darker blue-green glaze.

4. Fold the piece of brown paper carefully into four. Draw along the fold lines that have been created, using a straight edge and a pencil.

5. Draw diagonal lines from corner to corner through the middle of the folded lines.

6. Position the smallest circular template in the middle of the brown paper, accurately centred on the point where the lines cross. Draw your smallest circle.

7. Then place the second template over this and draw a second, larger circle.

8. Using a third and largest circular template, draw a third circle. These circles act as guidelines when you come to draw the star (see diagram 1). If

you cannot find exactly the right size circle, make a pair of compasses with string and pencil to draw your chosen size.

9. Using the circles as a guide, draw an eight-sided star with a pencil and straight edge (see diagram 2). The star tips should line up with the outer circle. The inverted inner points connect with the smaller circle.

10. With a steel rule and Stanley knife, cut along these lines to extricate the star shape.

11. Spray mount the back of the outer pattern of the star (not the star itself) and position it centrally on the table top.

12. Apply the forest green glaze with a dry stencil brush taking care not to allow the glaze to seep below the brown paper. When dry, repeat with the darker grey-green. While still wet, flick on spattered highlights of off-

white emulsion paint using an old toothbrush. Test and master this flicking movement on a scrap of paper first. Leave the star pattern to dry.

13. Using the brown paper as a template, cut out a shape for the remaining star shadow inset pieces (see diagram 3) and mark their position on the table top with fine pencil points.

14. Join these points with masking tape.

15. Stipple in a coat of mustard glaze. As you work, drop in a sprinkling of bronze or gold powder.

16. When dry, apply five coats of non-yellowing acrylic varnish to protect and seal the surface.

Fake trellis doors

Wooden trellis cupboard doors may look grand but they are expensive to purchase and also require endless dusting. Instead you can enjoy the rich quality of a trellis effect for the price of some paint and masking tape.

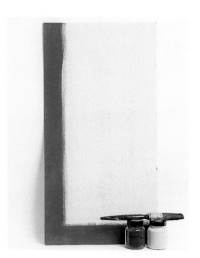

You will need:

Medium-grade sandpaper
Woodfiller (if your door surfaces are uneven)
Household paintbrushes
Deep terracotta, dark blue, bright ochre and white emulsion paint
Acrylic varnish
½in (1cm) wide masking tape
Pencil
½in (1cm) wide signwriter's tape
Small paint roller and tray

You can use an old cupboard with inset panels and mouldings like this one, but this idea also works for flat doors. For flat doors, you need to fake moulding and add a fine line of shading along either edge of the pretend moulding and a white line in the middle as a highlight. Depending on size, doors are often easier to decorate when unscrewed from their hinges and laid on to a flat surface. Like all paint effects, it is always wise to make up a test colour board first before tackling the main piece.

1. If you are using old doors, sand them first and fill any cracks and holes with woodfiller.

2. Paint the entire surface with the deep terracotta. When dry, sand down and varnish.

3. Mask a border 1in (2.5cm) inset from the outside of the door. Paint the outside patchily in dark blue so that some of the terracotta shows through. Paint the panel inside in pale yellow (made from mixing white with ochre). You may need two coats to achieve a good coverage.

4. With a pencil, mark 2in (5cm) spaces along all sides of the door front and then, using the marks as a guide, mask up the diamond trellis pattern with the signwriter's tape, working diagonally at a 45° angle and making sure the lines are straight and equally spaced between each line of tape.

5. With a small paint roller, apply yellow ochre emulsion over the trellis pattern. Leave to dry.

6. To make the shadows, mask diagonal lines ⅛in (3mm), away from the signwriter's tape with the masking tape. The lines should run diagonally across the doors from top right to bottom left. Paint the lines with pale blue (made from mixing the white with the dark blue emulsion). Leave to dry.

7. Remove the masking tape and mask off the lines in the other direction, ⅛in (3mm) away from the signwriter's tape. Note that the shadows occur on the two left hand sides of each diamond creating "V" shapes. Only two shaded lines are necessary.

8. Remove all the tape, leaving a ½in (1cm) border in terracotta all the way round. Seal with varnish for protection.

Faux marquetry table top

This is an ideal table top treatment if you are tired of plain pine or want to hide unsightly scorch marks. By using a stencilled pattern of simulated inlaid marquetry that is skilfully positioned, you can stencil over the top with wood-coloured crayons which will not obliterate the beauty of natural grain.

You will need:

Electric sander or medium- and
    fine-grade sandpaper
Ruler and pencil
Spray mount
Inlaid marquetry set stencil
Coffee-coloured stencil crayon

Black stencil crayon
Scrap paper
Stencil brushes
Heat- and water-resistant
    acrylic varnish
Houshold paintbrush

Like all the projects in this book, alternative colour schemes are open to all. This design can look good in two shades of green and in shades of purple and blue.

1. Sand away any stains and scorch marks but avoid making

the table top surface too uneven. Avoid sanding too vigorously – some table tops look solid but turn out to have only a thin veneer of real wood glued on to a thick chipboard base.

2. Using a ruler, find the middle

of the table and mark the centre with a light pencil mark. Draw two fine lines through this mark to divide the table neatly into four sections.

3. Spray mount the back of the stencil and place it in one of the quarters, making sure the right-angled corner butts accurately on to the centre mark.

4. Rub the stencil crayons on to a piece of paper using two different brushes, one for each colour. Pick up the crayon colour on the brush and rub it on randomly. Begin with coffee brown and finish with black.

5. Leave to dry for 24 hours and, when dry, protect with three coats of acrylic varnish.

Office chair transformation

For a fraction of the price of an upholstered armchair, this old office chair was transformed into a stylish and comfortable armchair by covering it with a simple button-on quilted throw.

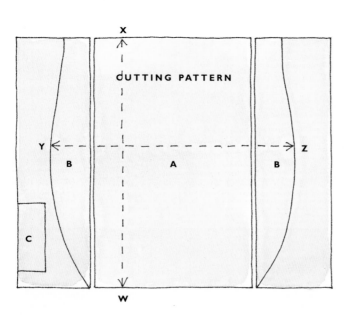

CUTTING PATTERN

DIAGRAM 1

You will need:

Office chair with arms and a gap
    between seat and back
Tape measure
Scissors
Upholstery fabric, 54in (137cm)
    wide, striped for easy quilting
Equal amount of light-weight
    Terylene wadding and lining
Sewing machine
Sewing thread and pins
Tailor's chalk
Six self-covered buttons

Because of the high cost of professionally made covers, informal throws for sofas and chairs are increasingly popular. Their only big drawback, unlike fitted covers, is that they are easily crumpled and dislodged. To avoid these common pitfalls, this design is buttoned down the back, which helps to keep it in place, and interlined with Terylene wadding, quilted along the stripes, which prevents creasing and adds weight.

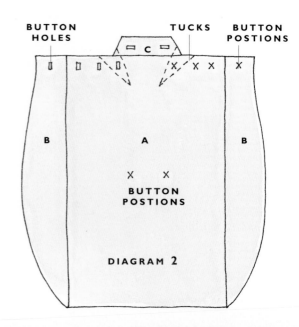

DIAGRAM 2

1. Following diagram 1 (see page 88), measure your chair from W to X and Y to Z to calculate your fabric requirements. Add a 1in (2.5cm) seam allowance all around. This measurement represents the size of your finished throw. Cut out the fabric, lining and wadding to these measurements. (The throw shown here needed approximately 5yds (5m) of fabric.)

2. Next, fold each piece of fabric, wadding and lining in half lengthwise to the W to X measurement. Cut along the fold of each piece.

3. Leave the lining to one side. Place the wadding on to the wrong side of both pieces of upholstery fabric. Pin and tack loosely together. One piece represents A on the cutting pattern (see page 88). Fold the other piece in half lengthwise and cut along the fold in order to make the B pieces. With tailor's chalk, draw the curved lines as shown, but do not cut out yet.

4. Cut out piece C on the cutting pattern to the same width as your chair and about 11in (28cm) deep. (The angles are cut later – at step 8.)

5. With right sides facing, machine stitch the fabric and wadding piece A to the two side pieces B. Open the seams and press. Then, with right sides facing, stitch piece C to the top middle of piece A (see diagram 2). Again, open and press the seam.

6. Fit the throw over the chair. Tuck the front into and through the gap in the back of the seat a little way, and pin temporarily to the middle of piece C.

7. Following the dotted lines on diagram 2, make two loose tucks in piece A, as shown, and pin.

Fold back the loose fabric behind the chair to form a "V" shape and mark the positions for the buttons and button holes with pins. Using the tailor's chalk line as a guide, work out a final hemline, marking it with a line of pins and making any necessary adjustments. The cover should just touch the floor.

8. Remove the cover and cut along this pin line. Cut away the excess fabric on piece C to angle the sides (see diagram 2).

9. Next, using the cover as a template, make up a lining to

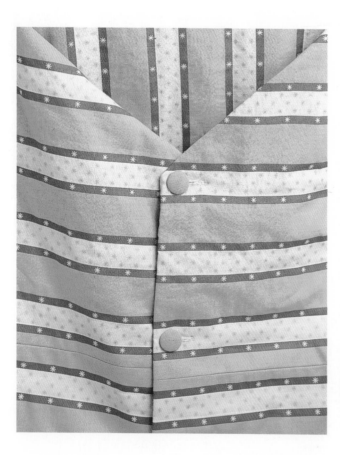
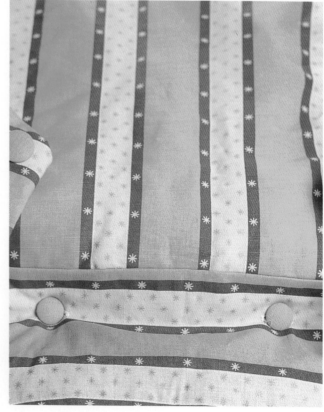

match, following the previous instructions for cutting and stitching. Pin to the back of the wadding and tack loosely in place to prepare for quilting. (The edges will be finished later.)

10. Quilt the chair cover by machine stitching parallel lines about 8–12in (20–30cm) apart, using the stripes on the fabric as a guide.

11. Make two button holes in piece C, about 6in (15cm) in from the side edges with a gap of about 8in (20cm) between them. Make button holes in one of the back flaps, following the positions marked with pins. Note the material of the back flaps is held folded in place by the button holes or buttons and so does not require stitching to secure.

12. Place the cover on to the chair for a final fitting to check the position of the buttons. Sew the buttons on to one back flap and on to the back of piece A (see the stars on diagram 2) so it can be buttoned to piece C.

13. For the bottom border, measure the perimeter of the cover and cut 6in (15cm) strips on the bias of the fabric. Join these into a continuous strip to the length of the perimeter measurement.

14. With right sides facing, place the raw edge of the strips 2in (5cm) in from the bottom of the

cover, tack and machine stitch (see diagram 3). Fold over as shown in diagram 4 and slipstitch. This bulky hemline enables the folds to splay and hang elegantly. Press the finished cover thoroughly and button on to the chair.

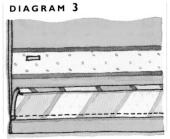

DIAGRAM 3

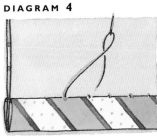

DIAGRAM 4

Mosaic table top

Stylish and hardwearing, a mosaic table top captures the essence of "al fresco" Mediterranean dining. Using ready-made glass tiles is an easy and inexpensive way of creating your own mosaic.

You will need:

Assorted sheets of glass squares (I used two sheets of white, two dark blue, two turquoise and one green)

A stable support surface (I used 1in (2.5cm) thick Medium Density Fibreboard (MDF), cut to 25 x 36in (63 x 91cm) square)

Pencil
Straight edge
PVA glue and brush
Tile grout
Grout spreader
Flat synthetic sponge

1. Soak the glass squares in water for about five to ten minutes to separate them from their paper backing.

2. Establish the centre of the table top by drawing two diagonal lines, from corner to corner. The centre is the point at which they intersect. Lay the tiles on to the table following the pattern shown here. Ensure the centre tile is laid over the pencilled cross. Leave narrow gaps between each piece for the grouting. This stage will take about two hours but it doesn't need to be done all at once. If you want to make up your own design, plan it out on paper first.

3. Once you know that all the pieces will fit, remove a small section at a time and brush the PVA glue on to the table top. Replace the tiles, checking that they are straight. Leave them to set overnight.

4. Mix up the tile grout according to the instructions on the package. It should have the consistency of thick soup. Apply generously over the surface of the tiles with the grout spreader.

5. Leave the grout for 15 minutes to dry but do not allow it to set. Gently wipe the surface of the mosaic with a slightly moist sponge to remove the excess grout. Keep the sponge flat to avoid removing the grout from between the tiles. Make sure the entire surface is clean before allowing the grout to dry fully.

6. Glue a row of tiles on to the edges of the support surface and when dry, grout as before.

Sofa divan transformation

It is a surprisingly simple project to transform a single divan bed into a comfortable sofa with the help of several large cushions, an elegant tasselled throw and a few basic sewing skills.

You will need:

A single divan with same size headboards at both ends. (This headboard is 33in (84cm) high.)

Electric drill

Two pieces of planed timber, 4 x 1in (10 x 2.5cm) and as long as the divan, plus the thickness of the headboards

Bradawl or skewer

Screwdriver

Eight 1½in (4cm) long screws

Tape measure

Scissors

Checked fabric and lining for cushion covers and three throws

Sewing machine

Thread and pins

Tassel fringing for one long edge of the bed cover and the outside edges of the two end throws between X and Y (diagram 2)

Four old pillows

Three floor cushions

Six large buttons

For easy conversion from a sofa into a bed, this design relies on three large cushions which are are thrown on to the floor at night and three throws, two of

which remain permanently in place and a seat throw which doubles up as a bedcover. A crease-resistant fabric is vital – a thick cotton or a lightly quilted fabric is ideal.

1. Drill two screw holes, 2in (5cm) apart, right through the wood at the ends of each planed timber piece. Position the timbers horizontally against the headboards to make a back stop for the large cushions. Allow for a gap between the timbers of about 6in (15cm) and position the top one a few inches below the height of the headboards. Make marks through the drilled holes using a bradawl or old skewer on to the side edges of the bed headboards. Screw the timbers in place.

2. Measure the length of the bed and the height of the mattress from the floor, and cut the main fabric and lining to make a seat cover. This should fit over the mattress and butt directly on to the floor. Add 12in (30cm) to the width so it can be tucked under the mattress at the back of the seat lengthwise, and add 24in (61cm) to the length so it can be tucked under the top and bottom end of the mattress.

3. With right sides facing, place the fabric on top of the lining and make a seam ½in (1cm) in from the raw edges all the way round, leaving a 12in (30cm) gap along the front bottom edge. Turn the right side out and press. Sew a tassel fringe along the bottom front edge.

4. To make the covers for the side arms, measure the width of the headboard (C on diagram 1), the distance between the top of the headboard and the floor (A on diagram 1), and the distance from the top of the headboard to the top of the mattress (B on diagram 1), adding 12in (30cm) for a tuck-in.

HEADBOARD WIDTH

DIAGRAM 1

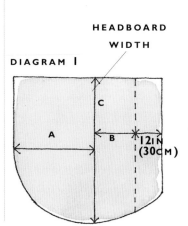

5. Cut out a square piece of fabric and lining to these dimensions. Place the checked fabric, right side up, on top of the lining and pin and tack together. Place this over the headboard, making sure that line C sits on the top ridge of the headboard. Pin and cut a curved bottom hem as in diagram 1.

6. Next, with right sides facing, machine stitch the fabric and lining together, following the instructions in Step 3. When the cover is turned the right side out and pressed, sew a tassel fringe to the front curved edge between X and Y (see diagram 2).

7. Make a second side arm cover, reversing the shape – as shown in diagram 2.

DIAGRAM 2

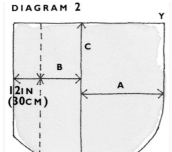

8. Place two pillows lengthwise together and stitch the covers together as near as possible to the edge. Do the same with the other two pillows. Position each pair with the seam butting on to the top ridge of the headboards at either end of the bed. Once covered with the throws, these cushions will be held firmly in place and provide the necessary bulk to create the arm shape.

9. Measure the floor cushions and cut a front cover for each, adding a 1in (2.5cm) seam allowance all round. Turn and hem along one of the raw edges.

10. Cut three back covers, adding a 1in (2.5cm) seam allowance, plus 6in (15cm) to one length. Turn in and hem the raw edges of the extended piece. Fold on to the wrong side of the fabric to make the same size as the front cover (see diagram 3).

11. Place the front and back cover on top of each other, right sides facing with the hemmed and folded sides together. Leave this side open and sew around the remaining three sides. Turn the cover the right way round and press.

DIAGRAM 3

12. Mark the positions for two button holes, equally spaced from the sides and from each other, along the hemmed opening of the cushion cover. Using the satin stitch gauge on your sewing machine, sew button holes. Sew buttons on to one thickness of the folded edge to match the position of the button holes and insert the cushions.

Fake inlaid marble

There is something about marble that is intrinsically splendid and it brings to mind the grandeur of European stately homes. Today it is possible to reproduce the effects with the help of some inexpensive paint products and simple techniques.

You will need:

Sandpaper
Old table top or piece of Medium
    Density Fibreboard (MDF)
Off-white vinyl silk emulsion paint
Pencil
Ruler or pair of compasses
Flexible masking tape
Low-tack masking tape
Sample board
Cotton buds
Water-based glazes in terracotta,
    sea coral, cream, grey and
    yellow
Paper plates

Household paintbrushes
Mutton cloth
Plastic wrap or plastic bag
Softening brush
Methylated spirits
Stippling brush
Small artist's paintbrush
Decorator's clear varnish

Although marbling sounds intimidating, it is not a difficult technique to master if you follow these simple short cuts. Instead of oil glazes, use water-based ones and substitute an ordinary artist's paintbrush for the traditional feather used for veining. As the right colour palette is crucial for convincing results, here is a botch-proof colour recipe. It helps to study examples of real marble if you want to experiment on your own. Remember that whilst some colours may be individually bright, once mixed, subtler colours will emerge. When marbling doors, you must work on them flat or the glaze will run.

1. Sandpaper your chosen surface. Then paint with two coats of off-white vinyl silk emulsion paint.

2. Once you've made sure the surface is flat, smooth and dry, draw a simple design on it with pencil. Depending on your design, you may need a ruler or pair of compasses, or you can use a large plate or bowl as a template.

3. Mask off the first area you aim to marble. Use flexible masking tape for curves and low-tack tape for straight lines.

Decide on an overall colour scheme, experimenting first on a small sample board. Tackle one area at a time and allow each area to dry for about 24 hours before applying masking tape to a neighbouring section. Although the glaze dries quickly (about one hour) it takes 24 hours to settle.

4. To create fake grouting between the marble inlays, place the masking tape a hair's breadth over an already-marbled area so that when you have marbled an adjoining area, you will be left with a dense dividing line. Or use a

cotton wool bud to push through the glaze to create a thin white dividing line (see the circle of the tray on page 101).

5. To create the marbling effect, pour a

small quantity of each colour on to a paper plate and, using a household paintbrush, apply one colour at a time in patches. Work the colour diagonally and vary the thickness of the brushstrokes.

6. Apply second, third and fourth colours in the same way, until the entire area is covered.

7. Fold a mutton cloth to form a smooth pad and dab the surface, picking up the excess glaze and creating a mottled effect.

8. Lay a piece of plastic wrap or a plastic bag over the wet surface and smooth with the palm of your hands. Peel off the bag carefully to reveal a "veined" texture left by creases in the bag.

9. Brush the wet glaze very lightly with a softening brush. When you use a softening brush, hold it at a 90° angle to the surface and make a swinging movement from the wrist – almost like applying loose face powder with a make-up brush.

10. Pour some methylated spirits on to a second plate. Load the stippling brush and dab it over the area. This will splatter the glaze and give the appearance of fossils. Then go over the area again with the softening brush.

11. To make marble look authentic it is not essential to add painted veins. An easy alternative is to simply push and twist a small artist's paintbrush through your work in a diagonal meandering fashion, always pushing the brush away from

you. It is also a good idea to emphasize and outline darker shapes by running the brush around them.

12. Soften the veins, using the softening brush in the same manner as before, and leave the glaze to dry.

13. To create a darker band of marble – mine is 2in (5cm) wide and set 6in (15cm) in from the outer edge – mask off with flexible masking tape and paint with grey and terracotta glazes. Allow random patches of the white base paint to show through and omit the veining process.

14. When you have completed the work, apply two coats of decorator's clear varnish. This helps to give the shiny appearance of real marble.

ALTERNATIVES

Cupboard top

The elegant inlaid marble top was created for a built-in cupboard using six pre-tinted glazes. The middle section is marbled in yellow, mint green and a dash of grey, the outer section is marbled in blue and emerald. The grey band was created by mixing pale and dark grey.

Marbled tray

Give an old wooden tray a remarkable new look by marbling in various shades of green. Decorated with four different pre-tinted glazes, the rim is painted in mint green and yellow, whilst a mixture of grey and emerald green has been used in the centre of the tray.

Tented shelving

Freestanding open shelving is the least expensive type of storage on the market – and, unfortunately, it can look as such. One way of upgrading cheap-looking shelving is to enclose it in fabric which has the added advantage of keeping it dust-free.

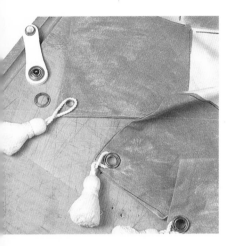  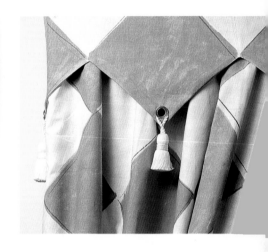

You will need:

Tape measure

Open shelf unit with a shelf at the very top of the unit

Scissors

Curtain wire plus eight screw eyes and hooks

Diamond-patterned fabric, measuring approximately 6½yds (6m)

Sewing machine

Iron-on tape

Large eyelets (enough for the pelmet, depending on the width and depth of your unit, plus eight for the curtain tie-backs)

Key tassels (about seven, depending on the width and depth of your shelf unit)

Ribbon, cord or contrasting fabric for tie-backs

Staple gun

1. Measure the height, depth and width of the shelf unit, and cut the curtain wire into four lengths – to fit the two sides and the front and back of the unit. Attach the screw eyes to the end of each length of curtain wire and fix the hooks (depending on your unit) to the edge or underside of the top shelf at either end of the unit sides, front and back. Stretch and fix the curtain wire rails into position.

2. To make the pelmet, cut two pieces of fabric 24in (61cm) wide and long enough to encircle the front and two sides of the unit, adding a 1in (2.5cm) seam allowance. Pin the two long pieces of fabric together, right sides facing, and machine stitch around the diamond pattern. Cut

the bottom edge of the fabric to follow the zig-zag shape of the diamonds. Trim away any excess fabric and snip into the seam allowance at the top of the Vs. Turn the fabric right side out and press. Fold in the top raw edges and seam with iron-on tape.

3. Following the instructions in the eyelet kit, position the eyelets along the bottom of the pelmet, one for each diamond. Before pushing in the second piece of the eyelet, attach the tassel loops as shown so that they are secured within the body of the eyelet.

4. Cut out the remaining fabric to make one back, two side and two front curtains to enclose the shelf unit. Using flat seams and with right sides facing join the

curtains together, leaving about 6in (15cm) at the top of each seam open, and leaving the two front curtains open. Fold over a small double hem along the top edge of each curtain to form a casing wide enough to accept the curtain wire. Machine stitch in place. Finish all raw edges using iron-on tape or machine stitch.

5. For the ties, position four eyelets in each curtain front, about 6in (15cm) apart. Make a thin ribbon out of a contrasting fabric to insert into the eyelets, or use ribbon or cord. Thread the ribbon and draw tight to pull the curtains back and tie in place.

6. Using the staple gun, attach the pelmet to the top edge of the shelf unit.

Faux malachite with gold leaf

Of all the semi-precious paint effects, malachite is one of the easiest to master with seriously glamorous results. A malachite effect mixed with gold leaf is an infallibly sumptuous combination and an ideal medium with which to decorate a range of small objects with classy and stylish results.

MALACHITE EFFECT

You will need:

Mint green vinyl silk emulsion paint
½in (1cm) wide paintbrush
Acrylic varnish
Low-tack masking tape
Artist's acrylic phthalo green,
 raw umber and French
 ultramarine
Acrylic scumble
Old plate (to use as a palette)
Small artist's paintbrush
Mutton cloth
Softening brush
Postcards
Decorator's varnish

1. Apply the mint green vinyl silk emulsion as the basecoat for your chosen item (in this case a picture frame) and leave to dry. Then seal it with acrylic varnish. When dry, mask off the four corners of the frame, which are to be gilded later.

2. Mix a thick glaze (about 80 per cent paint to glaze) using the phthalo green and scumble on your palette. Using the small paintbrush, patchily paint over the areas you want to decorate.

3. Next, mix a very small quantity of raw umber into the green glaze, just enough to darken the green. Use it to fill in some of the remaining patches.

4. Finally, mix a small amount of French ultramarine into the green glaze on your palette and paint in all the remaining spaces.

5. Fold over the mutton cloth into a smooth pad. Use it to dab over the wet glaze to eradicate the brush marks and remove any excess paint.

6. Use the softening brush to soften the effect and create a smooth finish.

7. To create the malachite shapes, cut the postcards into three or four strips of different widths, approximately 2 x 2in (5 x 5cm). Fold each strip and tear down the fold to make a rough, but straight edge. This will be the working edge. Use it to draw a half circle, applying even pressure on the wet glaze.

8. Draw another malachite shape lightly overlapping the first. Clean any excess paint off the card, and take a fresh piece of card when the first becomes soggy. Vary the circles in size using the different widths to add authenticity.

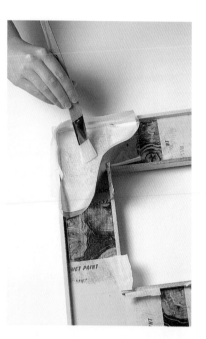

9. To recreate the tiny circular random crystals seen in real malachite, take a small artist's paintbrush and twist it in a circle to create small, round malachite formations in some of the dark spaces.

10. Using the artist's brush, draw a squiggly line around any of the remaining dark areas, following the shapes made by the card. Finally, when dry, soften the effect with a softening brush and seal with decorator's varnish. Leave to dry for 24 hours before applying the gold leaf (see opposite).

GILDING

You will need:

Low-tack masking tape
Small paintbrushes
*Wondersize (a special glue for
    Dutch Metal)*
*Dutch Metal (a gold leaf lightly
    secured to transfer paper)*

PVA glue
Gold powder
Acrylic varnish

1. Thoroughly mask off with tape the areas to which you have already applied the malachite effect – only when they are completely dry

2. Lightly brush the areas to be gilded with the size (glue).

3. Wait until the size is tacky to the touch (about 15 minutes), then peel a sheet of Dutch Metal from its backing, lay it over the size and rub over lightly with a small brush, allowing the excess size to flake away. Make sure the

area is thoroughly covered. Any corners which are hard to cover with the Dutch Metal can be touched up with a mixture of PVA glue and gold powder. Leave for 24 hours to dry.

4. Finally, seal with a coat of carefully applied acrylic varnish for protection.

Marbled table top with malachite inlay

For a really glamourous result, try using the malachite paint effect as an inlay on a fake marbled table top. The combination of malachite and marbling is quite stunning and easily achieved.

You will need:

*Medium Density Fibreboard (MDF)
  octagonal table top*
*1in (2.5cm) wide household
  paintbrushes*
Ivory white vinyl silk emulsion paint
Low-tack masking tape
Tape measure
Pencil
*Pre-tinted acrylic glazes in yellow,
  mint green and grey*
Plastic bag
Wallpaper or softening brush
*Items used for the malachite method
  (see pages 104–107)*

Here, marbling and malachite techniques combine to convert a piece of MDF into a spectacular table top. If you ask your timber merchant to cut you an octagonal table top, the effects are all the more impressive. You will need to refer back to the malachite technique on pages 104–107. Three paint techniques are used here: marbling in the centre, a malachite border and a "dragged" effect edge.

1. Paint the table with two coats of ivory white vinyl silk emulsion and leave to dry for six hours.

2. Using a low-tack tape, mask a 2in (5cm) border, set 4in (10cm) in from the outer edge of the table following the octagonal.

3. Using the mint green glaze, paint a border all the way round, dragging in one direction only, from the outer edge towards the masking tape. You should be able to see the brush strokes clearly.

4. Apply the yellow glaze with random brush strokes over the inside surface of the table encircled by masking tape. Add splodges of grey at random.

5. Spread a plastic bag over the wet glaze and iron it flat with your hand. Continue this process over the entire surface. This will leave a veined pattern which you can then soften with a wallpaper or softening brush. Leave to dry.

6. Reposition the masking tape to mask the outside edges of the border. Apply the malachite paint effect to the 2in (5cm) border, following the instructions on pages 104–107.

7. Apply two or three coats of acrylic varnish.

Weekend
Wonders

Like every aspect of life, the more time you invest, the more stunning the results. These projects fall into the category of requiring more dash than cash and, when completed, are ultimate proof of the validity of DIY. Be warned. Once you have experienced the thrill of transforming a room in a weekend, you could easily become a life-long addict.

- Lambrequin pelmet

- Concealed cupboards

- Stencilled bedlinen

- Director's chair cover

- Swedish sleigh bed

- Sofa cover

- Child's cabin bed

- Bathroom makeover

Lambrequin pelmet

If you live in a room overlooked by high windows or if you simply prefer an arched window to a square one, a lambrequin pelmet is the perfect solution. Its shape works perfectly with a simple roller or Roman blind.

You will need:

Measuring tape
Old sheeting and pins
Brown paper
Scissors
Pencil
Fretsaw
Plywood, ½in (1cm) thick
Checked fabric to cover the front and back of the lambrequin shape (see text)
Polyester wadding, 1in (2.5cm) thick
Bump interlining
Striped fabric to make the bias edging (see text)
Staple gun
Four shelf angle irons, 3in (7cm) long

The walls in this tiny bedroom were battened with 2 x 2in (5 x 5cm) timbers and then the same red checked fabric as the lambrequin was stapled to the timbers. Although this job takes time, it is not difficult. The lines of staples are hidden behind braid secured with fabric glue.

1. Take a measuring tape and measure your window width from the insides of the reveals.

2. Decide on a design that will suit your window. It may help to cut out the shape using an old piece of sheeting and to pin it in place to see whether you want to make any amendments to your chosen design.

3. Cut the brown paper to fit the window width and deduct ¼in (5mm) to allow for the thickness of the fabric. Estimate where the pelmet will end and cut the paper to this length. Fold the paper in half, draw half of your design

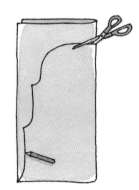

and cut out; open out.

4. Use a fretsaw to cut the plywood to the width and length of the paper and, using a sharp pencil, transfer the lambrequin design to the plywood. Cut out the design using a fretsaw.

5. Using the paper pattern cut out two pieces of the checked fabric, adding 2in (5cm) all the way around. Then cut the polyester wadding and bump interlining to the lambrequin shape as well.

6. Make a sandwich of the wadding, bump and the checked fabric, in that order, and lay over the plywood shape and staple to the back. Notch the curves to ease the fabric around the shape.

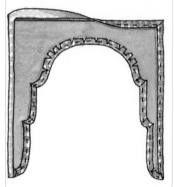

7. Cut 6in (15cm) thick bias binding from the striped fabric. With right sides facing, staple the bias 1½ in (4cm) in from the outside edge. Shoot the staples so that they butt together.

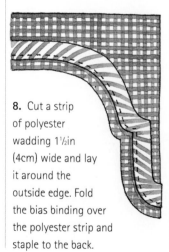

8. Cut a strip of polyester wadding 1½in (4cm) wide and lay it around the outside edge. Fold the bias binding over the polyester strip and staple to the back.

9. On right angled corners, cut and mitre the bias binding and fold under the raw edges. From the striped fabric, cut a 6in (15cm) long separate piece and mitre to cut across the corners. Staple in place.

10. Place the plywood board wrong side up, and cover the back with the second piece of fabric. Fold under the raw edges, and staple these to the back of the board.

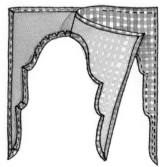

11. Screw four right angle brackets to the back of the lambrequin pelmet board, two at the top and two at each side, and screw the pelmet into the window reveal.

Concealed cupboards

In a bedroom, built-in wardrobes are often placed in the alcoves on either side of the bed. This can take up considerable space in a small room. An alternative is to build a slim, fake wall around a window and conceal the cupboards on either side.

You will need:

Graph paper and pencil
Spirit level and square
Handsaw
2 x 2in (5 x 5cm) planed timber to build your framework (see text)
Wallplugs, screw and toggle fixings for plasterboard walls
½in (12mm) Medium Density Fibre board (MDF) to build your doors and cladding (see text)
Hammer and nails
Surface-mounted concealed hinges (two per average size door)
Bradawl
Touch latches for cupboard doors

These 12in (30cm) deep cupboards, built to frame the window, create a deep sill and space at the sides of the window into which the bi-folding shutters are fitted. To make the shutters, see pages 66–67.

The timber framework is fixed to the walls, floor and ceiling, so check these are all sound and in good condition before attaching the timber. Also, check the position of any cables and pipes that need to be avoided. When fixing the framework directly on to the floorboards, make sure that the screws used are long enough to grip the board but not too long so as to endanger pipes and cables below. Before fixing the framework to the ceiling, locate a joist and mark its position to establish where the timber framework can be fixed.

1. Make an accurate plan on graph paper. Mark the position of the framework on the walls, floor and ceiling. Use a spirit level to ensure straight lines.

2. Using a handsaw, cut to length the planed timbers for the floor, ceiling and walls framework. When fixing timber to the ceiling, make sure you fix it to the joists for adequate support. Ensure all the timbers used are securely fixed in position.

3. Mark the position of the cupboard doors and fix the timber vertically to the framework to act as a support for the doors. Use a spirit level and square to ensure that the openings for the doors are square and that all the angles are true right angles.

4. Clad the timber framework, except for the door openings, with MDF cut to the appropriate size. Nail in place using a hammer. Make the doors to size.

5. Making sure they are straight and square, mark the positions for the concealed door hinges about 8in (20cm) in from the top and bottom of each door using a pencil.

6. Start the holes for the hinges with a bradawl. Reposition the hinges and screw to the edge of the door.

7. Place the hinges against the frame, mark the position of the screws as before; screw in place.

8. Attach touch latches to the doors. Decorate the cupboards to match the room and make them as inconspicuous as possible.

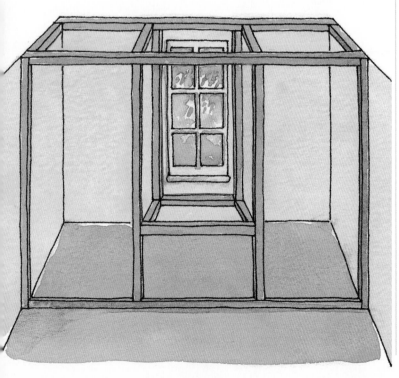

Stencilled bedlinen

Create a fresh country look with a white chintz bedspread and matching decorative pillowcases stencilled with pretty rows of leaves and rings of roses.

You will need:

White chintz fabric (if making your own pillowcase), the size of your pillow plus 1in (2.5cm) seam allowance, plus extra for a frill and flap (see text)
Masking tape
Flower garland and leaf stencils
Spray mount
Newspaper
Stencil spray paints in pink, yellow, green and grey-green
Card
Pins and thread
Sewing machine

Today's fabric paints and pens make it easy to stencil bedroom furnishings for delicate and original results. The spray paints used here produce a beautifully subtle shaded effect. Many paints will stand up to light washing or dry cleaning and even machine washing at a low temperature, but it is sensible to make up a

sample piece to test before you start. I have given instructions on how to make up a pillowcase.

1. Lightly secure the piece of fabric for the front of the pillowcase to a flat surface with masking tape. Smooth out any wrinkles but don't stretch it.

2. Secure the garland stencil to the centre of the fabric with spray mount.

3. Mask off any surrounding areas and parts of the fabric outside the protection of the stencil with sheets of newspaper.

4. Read the spray paint manufacturer's instructions carefully. After each spray, you may need to release the nozzle and, when finished, the spray button opening needs to be wiped. Spray on the pink colour first, directing the spray mainly on to the centre of the roses.

5. Spray the yellow paint on to the edges of the petals. As you do this, hold a piece of card so that it masks the pink in the centre of the rose. Only a light overspill from the spray should hit the fabric. Despite protection from the card, the colours will overlap a little, producing a soft, interesting texture quite unlike any shading achievable with solid paint. This is the effect to aim for.

6. Spray on a third colour, the green, directly at the leaves, then a fourth colour, the grey-green, again using the card. You should now have a subtle mixture of colour and texture. If you overspray, the fine dots, which give this technique its interesting texture, may disappear.

7. To make up the pillowcase, make up a 3in (7.5cm) scalloped frill to fit around the edge of the stencilled front pillowcase. Add 6in (15cm) for each of the

corners to allow for a pleated corner frill. Join the ends of the frill to make a circle.

8. With right sides facing, pin the frill to the raw edges of the front of the pillowcase. Pleat the corners. Tack in place and sew.

9. Cut an extra piece of fabric as wide as the pillow, 12in (30cm) long for the tuck-in flap. Place on to one end of the pillow front and seam on three sides.

10. Oversew the raw edges of the frill and pillowcase. Turn the right way round and press seams.

11. With right sides facing, place the pillow back on the front and seam around three sides leaving the folded side edge open. Turn the right way round and press.

12. Stencil the bedspread in the same way, using both the garland and the leaf stencil.

Director's chair cover

Transform old director's chairs into elegant and practical dining room chairs with a simply made smart new cover. Add a coronet hung with voile and you have the basis for an exotic tented dining room.

You will need:

Tailor's chalk, scissors and pins
2½ yds (2.5m) plain fabric per chair
Matching thread

Sewing machine with piping
* foot attachment*
Piping cord (see page 121 for
* instructions on how to*
* make your own)*

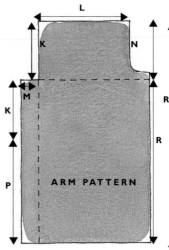

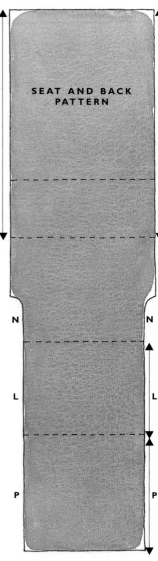

Measure your chair and follow the cutting patterns on this page. Cut the main body of the chair out as one piece. Cut one arm piece and the second arm in reverse. Add a seam allowance of ½in (1cm) and a hem of 2in (5cm). The measurements and quantities given below are sufficient for one chair cover.

1. Mark out and cut out the pieces with the grain of the fabric running lengthways. Take one arm piece and, with right sides facing, join flap K to both M and K to form the front of the arm cover. Fold along the dotted line and notch the corners to reduce the bulk. Repeat this sequence for the second arm.

2. Next, stitch the main body of the chair cover to the arm pieces.

With right sides facing, join seam P on the main chair cover to P on the arm cover, and then L to L and N to N. Repeat the process for the other arm.

ARM COVER

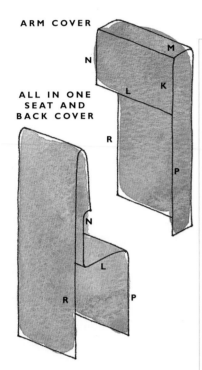

N

M
L K

ALL IN ONE SEAT AND BACK COVER

R

P

N

L

R

P

VOILE CORONET

You will need:

Scissors
8–12yds (8-12m) voile in two
colours
Tacking thread and pins
Matching thread
Sewing machine
Hula-hoop
Masking or parcel tape
(8yds) 8m matching ribbon
Cup hook
6 yds (6m) ivy or hops

3. Make up the piping cord in a contrasting colour, following the instructions opposite.

4. Pipe from the top of the chair back to the ground on both sides. Sandwich the piping between seams with all raw edges evenly aligned and right sides facing. Pin, tack and seam together.

5. The final seam, R to R, joins the back of the chair cover from the top of the arm downwards. With right sides facing, pin, tack and seam together.

6. Turn the chair cover the right way round and press. Finally, hem the raw edges all the way round the bottom.

The coronet voile tent is hung from a hula-hoop hung from the ceiling. To create the 'tent', the voile curtains can either be tied to hooks attached to adjoining walls, or held looped over the back of surrounding screens.

1. The length of the curtains will depend on the height of your ceiling. Cut fabric accordingly into four equal lengths.

2. On each piece make a ½in (1cm) hem and at the top edge, a single ½in (1cm) turn. Make a second 4in (10cm) turn along the top edge and stitch.

3. Sew parallel lines of stitching 2in (5cm) apart to provide the casing for the hoop, leaving a frill at the top edge of each piece.

4. Cut the hoop and slide it into the fabric casings, alternating the coloured lengths of voile. Rejoin

the hoop with tape and hide the join inside one of the casings.

5. Attach the hoop to the ceiling with lengths of plain ribbon tied at four equal points. Hold the coronet level and tie the ribbons together about 3ft (1m) from the hoop. Fix to a cup hook screwed

into a ceiling joist or tie to any light fitting that is fixed to the ceiling with a chain. Never attach directly to an electrical cable.

6. Wind the ivy or hops around the inside and outside of the hoop, intertwining with ribbons to secure.

PIPING FOR ONE CHAIR COVER

You will need:

Fabric in a colour to contrast with the chair cover
Scissors
Sewing machine with piping or zipper foot attachment
Thin piping cord

Although not essential, these chairs look even more stylish with the addition of piping in a contrasting colour.

1. To make piping, always cut the fabric on the bias grain so it can stretch. Lay the fabric out with the selvedge edges left and right. Fold the fabric along a 45° angle to create a triangle. You now have a true diagonal from which to cut your strips of fabric.

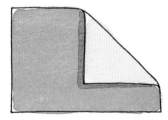

2. Cut along the fold and then cut parallel strips approximately 2½in (6cm) wide.

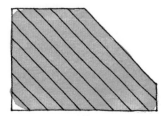

3. To join the strips of fabric, place the right sides together and stitch ¼in (5mm) in from the raw edges. Note the 45° angle that the seam produces.

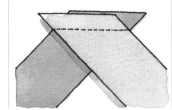

4. Press open the seams and clip the corners as shown.

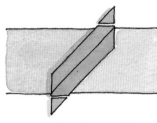

5. Wrap the binding around the cord with wrong sides facing enclosing the cord. Tack to hold in place. Using the piping or zipper foot, machine stitch as close as possible to the cord. The finished piping can now be sandwiched between the two pieces of the chair cover and stitched in place within the seam.

You will need:

Brown paper and pencil

A single size divan

For the sides, two pieces of ¾in (20mm) thick Medium Density Fibreboard (MDF), cut 24in (61cm) high and to the same length as the divan frame plus 4in (10cm)

Scissors

Spray mount

For the top and bottom ends, two pieces of MDF, ¾in (20mm) thick, 37in (95cm) high, cut to the same width of the divan frame plus 4¾in (12cm)

Jigsaw and sandpaper

Electric drill

Four pieces of 2 x 2in (5 x 5cm) timber, cut to the divan width, less 6in (15cm) (B on diagram 1)

Four pieces of 2 x 2in (5 x 5cm) timber cut to the divan length, less 6in (15cm) (A on diagram 1)

Screws and screwdriver

Eight 2 x 2in (5 x 5cm) timbers cut to 6in (15cm) lengths

Four round ball cupboard feet

Four spindle knobs

3in (7.5cm) screws

Wood glue

Household brushes

Dark forest green and emerald green emulsion paint

Stencil

Stencil paints and brushes

Acrylic varnish

1. Make a paper template the same height and half the length of one MDF side piece and draw on to the paper half the shape to be sawn out. Cut out the paper pattern with scissors.

2. Using spray mount, fix the pattern on an MDF side piece, to line up with the middle of the bed. Using a pencil trace around the template. Reverse the pattern and repeat the process.

3. Using the same method, draw out the shape for the other side, the head and foot of the bed.

4. With a jigsaw, cut all four pieces along the pencilled lines and sand the raw edges.

5. Drill holes in pieces B (see diagram 1). Locate the position of the timber frame within the divan and screw two B battens

Swedish sleigh bed

Here is a simple way to transform a single divan into an imaginative sleigh bed.

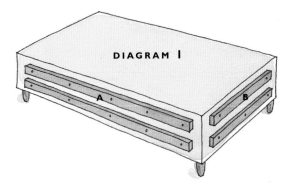

DIAGRAM 1

DIAGRAM 2

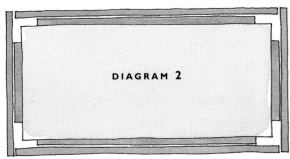

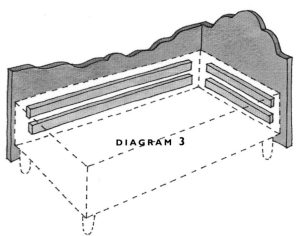

DIAGRAM 3

DIAGRAM 4

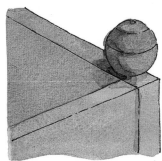

DIAGRAM 5

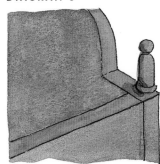

two long sides, headboard and footboard in place to form a box (see diagrams 2 and 3).

7. The eight 6in (15cm) timber lengths act as bases for the ball feet (see diagram 4) and the spindle knobs (see diagram 5). Screw these lengths into the upper and lower corners of the frame. Glue the spindle knobs to the upper supports and screw the ball ends to the lower ones.

8. Paint the MDF frame in dark green emulsion paint. When dry, paint over with a 50:50 mix of the emerald green emulsion and water, which will allow some of the base colour to show through. Leave to dry.

9. Apply a stencil of your choice. As a guide, you can follow the photographic step-by-step sequence above.

10. Cover with a coat of acrylic varnish for protection.

horizontally across the bedhead and base end of the divan. Repeat this process for the A battens.

6. Mark and screw holes in the headboard and base end to line up with the battens. Screw the

123

Sofa cover

Making a loose cover for a sofa is time consuming but not as difficult as it might appear. It not only saves money but also presents you with the opportunity of creating your own distinctive fabric style. This white sofa cover is specially designed for a seaside home and is suitably trimmed in nautical blue, turquoise and white striped bias binding to match the stool and cushion covers.

You will need:

Tape measure
Tailor's chalk
For a two-seater, approximately 12–14 yds (12-14m) furnishing fabric; for a three-seater, approximately 14–16 yds (14-16m) of fabric. The fabric should be 55in (137cm) wide, closely woven and pre-shrunk
Scissors
Pins
Needle
Piping cord
Bias binding
Sewing machine with piping or zipper foot attachment
Matching sewing threads
Sturdy zip for sofa cover
Zips for cushion seat covers

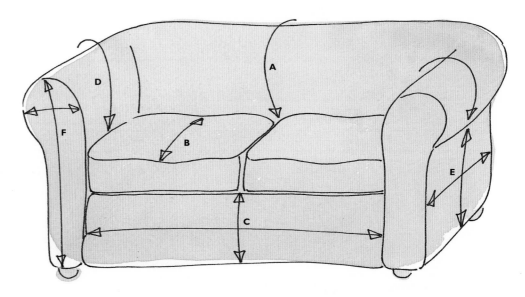

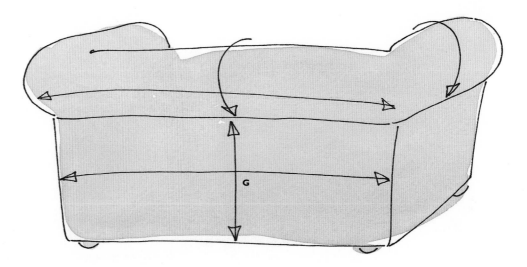

MEASURING UP

When measuring up for your sofa cover, remember to add ¾in (2cm) seam allowances all around where instructed, and 6in (15cm) tuck-ins to go in the gaps around the seat to prevent strain. Following the diagram on page 124, measure the following:

A Inside Back – width and depth from the lower edge of the scroll back to the seat, plus a tuck-in and seam allowances.

B Seat– width and depth, plus tuck-ins on two short and one long side, and seam allowances.

C Front – width and depth plus seam allowances.

D Inside Arm (cut two) – width and depth, from the lower edge of the scroll back to the seat, plus tuck-in and seam allowances.

E Outside Arm (cut two) – width and depth plus seam allowances.

F Front Arm (cut two) – width and depth plus seam allowances.

G Outside Back – width and depth plus seam allowances.

CUTTING OUT

Following the measurements, mark cutting lines along the grain of the fabric, making sure each piece sits squarely. Cut out the pieces. Mark the relevant letter on each piece. You may need to join fabric to make the required width of pieces A, B, C and G. To avoid making a central seam, centre each piece across the full width of the fabric and, matching the pattern, join an extra piece to each side. Label each piece for easy identification.

Cut four pieces of fabric 12in (30cm) wide by 8in (20cm) deep for the mock pleats.

MAKING UP

1. Make up enough piping (see page 121) to fit around the front arms, twice around each cushion and along the bottom edge and front of the sofa (optional).

2. On the sofa, mark a chalk line down the centre of the outside back G, the inside back A, the seat B and the front C. Repeat on the wrong side of the corresponding fabric sections, folding them in half to find the middle. With the wrong side of fabric uppermost, pin the outside back piece G to the back of the sofa. Align the top edge to fit along the base of the scroll back (see diagram 1).

DIAGRAM 1

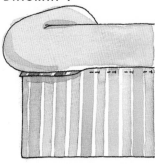

3. Next, position and pin inside back piece A, wrong side uppermost, with the tuck-in at the lower edge. Trim piece A to form a mitred corner across the scroll shape at each side of the piece and make notches into the seam allowance to form a curve (see diagram 2).

DIAGRAM 2

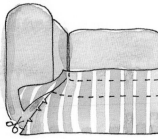

4. Along the back of A, make pleats to fit around the scroll. Pin and tack (see diagram 3). With right sides facing, pin A to G along this line of tacking. Remove pins to do so, where necessary, but do not remove pieces from the sofa. Tack together. With right sides facing, pin and tack A to seat piece B at the lower edge of the tuck-ins. Remove the cover and machine along the tack lines.

DIAGRAM 3

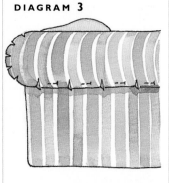

5. Replace the cover on the sofa, wrong side up. With right sides facing, fit, pin and tack the two D pieces to the E pieces, ensuring the joining seams sit just below the rolled edge of the arm. Mitre and trim the D pieces to fit into the corner and shape over the arm to join the mitred edges of A. Clip into the seam allowance of

the curves so they fit snugly over the scroll (see diagram 4).

DIAGRAM 4

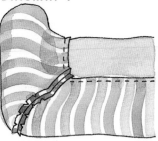

6. With right sides facing, pin and tack the D pieces to A; pin and tack the bottom of the D pieces to B at the lower edge of the tuck-ins. With right sides facing, pin and tack the outside back piece G along one side edge to one E piece. At the other end, leave a 24in (61cm) opening between G and E for the zip.

7. Arrange the D pieces to fit around the front edges of the arms by making small pleats, about 2in (5cm) deep. Pin and tack to secure. With tailor's chalk or loose tacking, mark the curved seat seamline, following the arched shape (see diagram 5). Trim the excess fabric. With right sides facing, pin and tack seat piece B to front piece C. Make sure the join sits along the front edge of the sofa seat. Remove the sofa cover.

8. Position the front arm pieces F the wrong side up. Mark the seamline with pins and a line of tacking. Trim to shape (see diagram 6).

DIAGRAM 5

DIAGRAM 6

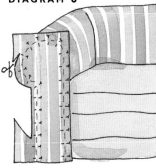

9. Remove the front arm pieces and tack piping around them, right sides facing. Then, pin and tack the front arms to pieces D, C and E, with right sides facing, and with the piping sandwiched in between the seams. Leave open 7in (18cm) at the lower outer edge of each front arm F piece for a mock pleat. Bind the raw edges of the openings with bias binding. Remove the cover and machine stitch along all the lines of tacking.

10. Replace the cover, right side out. Turn in, pin and tack the raw edges of the back opening to make a seam line for the zip. Pin and tack one side of the zip in place. If you are piping the

bottom edge of the cover pin and tack piping in place with the raw edges together. To make the pleats, place two pleat pieces together, right sides facing and machine stitch along two short and one long side. Trim the corners, turn right side out and press. Repeat to make the other pleat. Pin the short sides of each pleat to E and F in the opening at each corner to line up with the hemline.

11. Remove the cover. Pin and tack and machine stitch the remaining side of the zip. Stitch the piping along the hemline and fold back the raw edges. Bind with bias binding and hem on the wrong side. On the inside, top stitch the pleat piece to the main body of the cover by hand.

12. Measure up for the seat cushions. Cut two pieces of fabric for the top and bottom of each cushion, including all the seam allowances.

13. For the gusset, cut a strip of fabric the depth of the cushion pad and long enough to encircle three sides of the cushion. Cut a strip for the gusset zip section. This should be the length of one side of the cushion, plus 4in (10cm), so that it extends around two corners. Add 1¼in (3cm) to the depth for pressed edges either side of the zip. Cut the zip section in half lengthways and press the seam allowances. Tack the zip between the pressed

edges and machine. Stitch one edge of the zip section to one short edge of the main gusset.

14. Pin one cushion cover piece to the gusset strip, with right sides facing and with the piping sandwiched in between. (Ensure the zip is centred in the side of

the cushion that will be facing the back of the sofa.) Trim the gusset to fit and join the short raw edges. First tack, then machine the gusset to the cover piece. Open the zip and join the gusset to the other cover piece in the same way. Finally, turn the cushion cover right side out..

Child's cabin bed

An imaginative addition to a narrow child's room is a bed cabin that can be tucked into the darker end, creating a snugly curtained-off room within a room. Well lit with spotlights, this design is styled to look like a small theatre.

You will need:

Single divan and mattress without
    headboard
Handsaw
2 x 2in (5 x 5cm) planed timber for
    the framework (see text)
Wallplugs, screw and toggle fixings
    for plasterboard walls
Spirit level, straight edge and pencil
Screws of various sizes and
    screwdriver
½in (1cm) thick MDF boards to
    enclose the sides and back
¾in (2cm) thick Medium Density
    Fibreboard (MDF) boards to
    enclose the front and ceiling
Scissors and brown paper
Pair of compasses and plate
Jigsaw
Wood glue
Tongue and groove boards to clad
    the front of the cabin
Power file
Decorative dado rail
Curtain poles or wire
Limed oak white wash or your
    chosen paint
Household paintbrush

This idea works well in most small rooms, even if the room is wider than the length of a single bed, as the difference can be taken up by a shelf built about 12in (30cm) above bed height, which makes a useful pillow stop and a space for

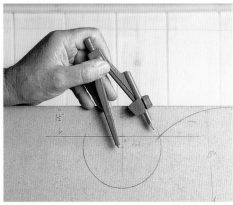
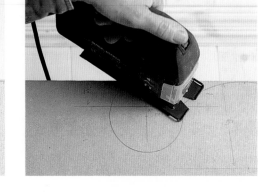

books and toys. The cabin is made from MDF cladding fixed to battens screwed to three surrounding walls and the floor. Before beginning the project, ensure the walls and ceiling are in good condition and check on the position of cables and pipes which need to be avoided. Fixing battens to the floorboards is usually possible, although screws should only be long enough to grip the floorboards, unless there is a convenient joist below. The divan slots into the space before the front is screwed in place. Make an accurate plan on graph paper to work out quantities of materials required.

1. According to your plan, buy or saw the lengths of timber to make a framework for the cabin shown in this drawing.

2. Mark the position of the battens on the walls using a spirit level, straight edge and pencil. Screw the battens in place. Cut the base of the uprights to fit

around the skirting boards. Screw in a batten to span the front top of the bed frame from wall to wall and fix the framework to support the shelf and headboard.

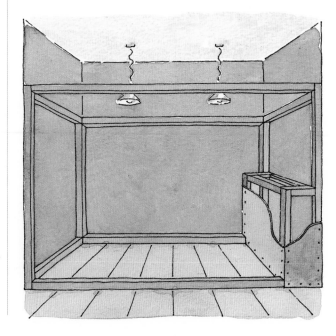

3. Cut the MDF boards for the three inside walls to the required size and screw to the battens.

4. Saw the MDF boards to the required size for the back and top of the bedhead shelf. Screw on to the batten framework. Now you can put the divan into position.

5. For the front of the cabin, cut two pieces of MDF to fit together vertically. Draw and then cut a large opening, mattress-height

off the floor, to the length of the bed and at least 5ft (1.5m) high – high enough for a child not to bump his or her head when getting in and out of bed.

6. For the shaped cornice, cut a piece of brown paper 12in (30cm) wide and measuring half the width of the bed.

7. Use a pair of compasses and a plate to draw the shape; cut this out of the brown paper. Draw

around the template on to one sheet of MDF and then reverse it to complete outlining the design on the other half of the bed top. Cut out with the jigsaw.

8. To clad the front of the bed, roughly shape, glue and tack the tongue and grove cladding on to the MDF front and, when secure, carve to shape with a power file.

9. For the ceiling, cut the MDF to size; screw on to the top of the

frame. Cut holes for halogen spots and have an electrician install these and a two-way switch from the bed to the door.

10. Cut a length of decorative dado rail to attach to the top of the bed cabin. Fix curtain poles or curtain wire inside the structure to hang curtains around all four sides of the bed cabin.

11. Apply a limed oak white wash or paint as you like.

Bathroom makeover

If your bathroom looks tired and dull, but does not merit new fixtures, here is a fabric and paint effect recipe that will give it almost instant new life without costing too much. The fabric awning in blue and beige dictated the colour scheme.

TONGUE AND GROOVE CLADDING

You will need:

Household paintbrushes
Off-white vinyl silk emulsion paint
Dado rail
Straight edge, spirit level and pencil
1in (2.5cm) wide masking tape
Panel pins and hammer
Try square
¼in (6mm) wide signwriter's tape
Honey pine and grey pre-tinted glaze
Woodgrainer
Old cloth
Softening brush
Blue emulsion paint
Carpenter's pencil
White crayon
Acrylic varnish

Instead of looking cramped, a small space can be made to look cosy and well-ordered. In this bathroom, an imperfect ceiling and pipes were hidden behind a fabric awning slung between poles and extended to line up with the top of the window. Old bland white tiles were removed and replaced by fake tongue and groove boarding. Combined with the fake floor tiles, this gave the room a rustic character.

When faking the boarding and the tiles, you can paint directly on to existing plaster and floorboards unless, as in this room, the walls are too uneven and the floorboards not worth sanding, in which case inexpensive plywood sheets provide a clean

flat lining. New shutters were painted in blue to match the fabric, and the pine accessories were painted in the same blue, diluted with water to make a wash which coloured but did not obliterate the grain. The fake boarding was also washed in the diluted blue emulsion paint.

1. Paint the walls in off-white vinyl silk emulsion. Leave to dry.

2. Decide on the height of your dado rail and, with the help of a straight edge and spirit level pencil a straight horizontal line to encircle the room. Use the masking tape to mask above the line. Cut the dado rail to size and fix on to the wall with the panel

pins directly below the masking tape. Paint the dado rail in the off-white emulsion.

3. From the floor up to the dado rail, measure and mark in pencil 6in (15cm) wide gaps to define the gaps between tongue and groove boarding. Pencil vertical lines using the straight edge and a try square for accuracy.

4. With the signwriter's tape, mask the vertical lines.

5. Using one brush for each glaze colour, apply the honey pine and grey glazes patchily over one fake plank at a time, working in a vertical direction. Paint the dado rail similiarly.

6. Pull the wood grainer through the wet glazes, rocking the roller slightly at intervals but in one smooth motion. Work one "plank" at a time and vary the pattern of the graining between the planks as much as possible. Make some quite plain by reducing the rocking action of the grainer. Remove any excess glaze from the rocker with an old cloth.

7. Pull the softening brush over the boards to blur the effect.

8. When the glazes are dry apply a coat of blue emulsion paint thinned with 50% water. When dry, remove the signwriter's tape.

9. To emphasize the edge of each plank, use the carpenter's pencil to draw two thick parallel lines either side of the groove. In between draw a line of white using an ordinary child's crayon.

10. To protect the paint effect, apply a coat of acrylic varnish.

COLOURWASHING THE WALLS

An off-white basecoat is first applied to the walls. Using the same colour glazes that were used for the boarding, dab them alternately on to the walls with an ordinary brush. Then rub over with an old cloth to achieve a soft colourwashed effect. The skirting boards, window sill and doors can be treated in the same way. The cupboard doors were simply painted to match the tongue and groove boarding.

TENTED CEILING

You will need:

Fabric for ceiling plus tape measure, sewing machine, thread, scissors and pins
Bobble fringe
Rail sockets and screws

Curtain poles (or dowelling) cut to the width of the ceiling,

1. Measure the width and length of the ceiling, adding about 24 in (60cm) to the length for the overhang. Cut out your fabric. Using flat seams, join the fabric widths together. Press seams open. Neaten all edges with a small double hem. Pin and stitch the bobble fringing to two edges.

2. Screw the rail sockets into position (here we used three on one wall and three on the opposite wall). Slot the poles into the sockets. Finally place the fabric over the poles.

FAKE COUNTRY TILES

You will need:

Household paintbrushes
Off-white vinyl silk emulsion paint
Steel rule
Pencil
¼in (6mm) wide signwriter's tape
Two pre-tinted glazes in
    Mediterranean blue and
    aquamarine
Plastic bags
Softening brush
Acrylic varnish

1. Paint the floor with two coats of off-white vinyl silk emulsion paint and leave to dry.

2. Using the steel rule, measure and pencil 10in (25cm) square tiles or any size to suit your floor.

3. Divide the squares with tape.

4. Using a separate paintbrush for each colour, dab the two glazes on to the floor, maintaining a definition between the colours.

5. While the glazes are still wet, place a plastic bag over the

surface and smooth flat, pressing down with your hand. Lift the bag off straight away. The bag will leave behind a randomly

textured marble effect (see above) across the floor. Gently soften the effect with the use of a softening brush.

6. When dry, lift off the signwriter's tape. Apply three coats of acrylic varnish to the floor for protection.

Ingenious ideas

Everybody loves a new and clever idea that can be tackled in a matter of minutes. Here are some of the most useful and spectacular using flowers, paints and fabrics. Some take longer than others, but they are all extremely decorative, effective and relatively easy.

- Decorative doors

- Sheer delights

- Floral tricks

Decorative doors

Behind every tired cupboard door is a wealth of decorative possibilities just waiting to be explored. Here are some of the most reliable paint effect recipes. All require a vinyl silk emulsion paint base to seal the surface, over which glazes can be manipulated, and all need protecting with a coat of varnish.

1. Apply a coat of antique pine wood dye, leave to dry, rub over it patchily with a candle and paint in a traditional grey-green colour. Finally soften the edges between the pine and paint with an old cloth.

2. Strip off old varnish and brush with a wire brush in the direction of the grain. Mix equal measures of water and white emulsion paint and apply. Finish off with a stencilled wreath in autumnal colours.

3. Paint two tones of glaze, minty green and tropical blue, over an off-white vinyl silk base. While still wet, dab over them with a stippling brush, swirling the brush, but keeping the colours separate.

4. For a dramatic effect, randomly apply four glazes mixed with artist's colours – chrome yellow, alizarin crimson, burnt umber and Mars black – on to a cream base. While wet, flick and drag with an old cloth.

5. Rather than removing old varnish to expose real wood grain, the lazy alternative is to paint a plain vinyl silk base in grey or green and then, with a woodgrainer, to create a limewashed wood effect using white emulsion paint mixed with clear glaze.

6. An inlaid stone effect can look extremely classy and is easily done. Apply a basecoat of off-white emulsion paint. Follow the pattern above by drawing a diamond within a rectangle. Mask the sections and stipple them in four sophisticated shades of green and grey, waiting for each section to dry before remasking.

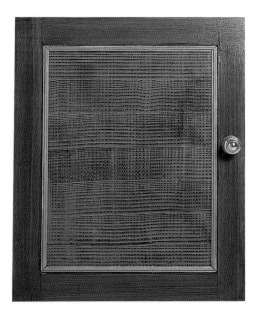

7. This interesting woven texture was created with a decorator's comb. First, the door was given a basecoat of lilac vinyl silk emulsion paint. When dry, it was painted with a mixture of one part artist's acrylic alizarin crimson to six parts glaze. Then the comb was worked over the wet glaze in criss-cross directions. The sides were dragged in the same glaze over a darker base and the moulding was painted gold.

8. This faux Sienna marble was made using artist's oil colours – chrome yellow, raw sienna, burnt sienna, alizarin crimson, burnt umber and Mars black painted on to an off-white eggshell base. Each colour was mixed separately with an oil glaze and painted in a meandering diagonal line. The veining was created with a feather dipped in brown and then softened with a softening brush.

Sheer delights

Voile is a wonderfully versatile fabric and ideal for no-sew window treatments. You can scrunch it, wrap it, knot it, wind it, thread it through curtain rings and nine times out of ten it will hang stylishly whatever you do. Add shutters or a blind and you have the ultimate no-sew window treatment.

1. This sleek and simple arrangement is perfect for a pair of windows or in a room where there is more space on one side of the window than the other. Start with a large knot at one end of the pole and then swag the fabric in one big swoop and thread over the opposite finial, allowing the overspill voile to pool on to the floor.

2. This romantic treatment owes its success to the decoratively shaped edge of an exquisite cotton lace. The fabric is folded in half lengthwise and then in half widthwise to find the middle, where it is bunched loosely along the folded edge. It is held with an elastic band to form a rosette. Fabric on either side of the rosette is stretched and tucked behind each end finial and held with a curtain clip. The rosette is stretched outwards to form a fan shape and then secured with extra clips.

3. To create these sumptous swags, simply combine a layer of checked sheer fabric with a layer of sheer striped fabric. Slot the fabric through curtain rings and arrange as you like. This treatment looks good combined with a roller blind which provides privacy and controls the amount of light allowed in.

4. Here, two scarf lengths of checked sheer fabric edged with tartan ribbon are softly draped over the pole to create independent swags which are then tied loosely together in the middle like a scarf. Combine with a pair of full-length voile curtains to complete the translucent visual theme.

To calculate how much voile to buy, use a length of piping cord or any thick string and arrange it over the pole, following the shape you plan to create with voile. Cut and measure and work out the length to the nearest yard or metre. If you want to cut a tail on the diagonal, allow for extra fabric. If in doubt, first cut out your shape using an old sheet. For a long classic tail, cut the end at a 45° angle and, for a sharper modern look, cut the ends straight across.

1

2

3

4

Floral tricks

Nothing compares with the impact of a bunch of flowers, imaginatively arranged, to put new life into a room. Here are eight quick and easy ways to make a dazzling show.

1. For an instant vase, cut a plastic water bottle in half, wrap it in coloured tissue paper and cellophane and tie with raffia. Fill with water and flowers of your choice.

2. Turn a cabbage head into an unusual vase by scooping out the centre, concealing a container within it, and filling with water and tulip heads. Place the entire arrangement on a pedestal bowl.

3. For a tiny indoor garden, plant a silver mesh trug with violets and ferns. Line the mesh with moss or transparent polythene. As the container may not be fully waterproof, remember to place on a saucer before watering.

4. Create an unusual arrangement by teasing the flower-heads – here tulips – into a dome shape. Tie just below the flowers with string. Cut the stalks to the same size and fit into a water container concealed within an oasis block covered in moss and placed in a pot.

5. Narcissi and spring twigs apparently grow in a neat row. In reality, they are held in an oasis block encased in a layer of plastic sheeting. This in turn is covered with magnolia leaves tied with raffia.

6. Make a stem vase by cutting flower stalks to the same height as an empty soup tin. Glue the stalks around the tin and secure with raffia. Fill the tin with water and flower-heads.

7. This arrangement makes a strong geometric statement. Tie together autumnal flowers and foliage and place them in a glass cube vase. Make sure the stems look neat as they are as visually important as the flower-heads.

8. Cover a round oasis ball with moss using florist's wire bent into hair-pin shapes. Slot on to a pre-cut thick twig. Stick into a dry oasis block hidden under more moss in a pot. Decorate the moss ball with chocolates wrapped in silver paper, if liked, secured with wire.

Index

A

analogous colour schemes, 13
armchairs, transformed office
    chairs, 88–91

B

bamboo, picture frames, 52–3
bathrooms, makeovers, 130–3
bedlinen, stencilled, 116–17
beds
    child's cabin, 128–9
    Swedish sleigh, 122–3
blinds
    handpainted, 50–1
    seersucker, 42–3

C

cabin beds, 128–9
ceilings, tented, 130–2
ceramics
    painted plates, 30–1
    painted terracotta pots, 31
    place names, 16–17
chairs
    director's, 118–21
    stencilled, 74–5
    transformed office, 88–91
chicken wire, cupboard doors,
    70–3
children's beds, 128–9
china cupboards, fake, 70–3
clover leaf shutters, 66–7
coffee tables
    faux inlaid granite, 80–3
    stools from, 76–7
colour schemes, 10–13
    analogous, 13
    complementary, 12
    contrasting, 12
    harmonious, 13
    monochrome, 11

neutral, 11
white and favourite colour, 12
colour sense, building, 10
complementary colour schemes,
    12
consoles, antique-style, 54–5
contrasting colour schemes, 12
cupboards
    decorative doors, 136–7
    doll's-house, 44–5
    dressers, 62–3
    fake, 70–3
    fake trellis doors, 84–5
    Gustavian style, 40–1
    trompe l'oeil, 70–3
curtains, goblet-headed, 60–1

D

decoupage firescreens, 68–9
director's chair, covers, 118–21
divans, transforming, 96–7
doll's-houses, cupboards, 44–5
doors
    decorative, 136–7
    fake trellis, 84–5
dressers, trompe l'oeil, 62–3
dressing tables, Gustavian-style,
    48–9

E

equipment, 6–9

F

fabrics
    blinds, 42–3, 50–1
    curtains, 60–1
    director's chair covers,
        118–21
    lambrequin pelmets, 112–13
    pencil pots, 20–1
    photo frames, 20–1

sewing box, 18
sofa covers, 124–7
sofa divans, 96–7
tented ceilings, 130–2
tented shelving, 102–3
transformed office chairs,
    88–91
voile drapes, 138–9
window screens, 46–7
fake effects
    granite inlay, 80–3
    inlaid marble table tops,
        98–101
    malachite inlay, 108
    malachite with gold leaf,
        104–7
    marquetry, 86–7
    trellis doors, 84–5
    tongue and groove cladding,
        130–1
    see also paint effects
fan blinds, seersucker, 42–3
faux effects see fake effects
finger-painting, trays, 22–3
firescreens, decoupage, 68–9
flower decoration, 140–1
flowerpots
    painted, 30–1
    place names, 16–17
    stencilled designs, 32–3
frames
    candelabras, 36–7
    fabric, 20–1
    faux malachite, 104–7
    flower vase, 26–7
    oriental bamboo, 52–3
    vinegar-painted, 34–5
frosted windows, stencilled, 32–3
furniture, distressed look, 12

G

gilding, 107
glass tiles, mosaic table tops,

92–5
goblet-headed curtains, 60–1
gold leaf, with faux malachite,
    104–7
granite inlay, faux, 80–3
Gustavian-style
    cupboards, 40–1
    dressing tables, 48–50

H

harmonious colour schemes, 13

I

inlaid granite, faux, 80–3
inlaid marble, fake, 98–101

L

lambrequin pelmet, 112–13
lampshades, paper, 24–5
loose covers, sofas, 124–7

M

malachite, faux, 104–7, 108–9
marble
    fake inlaid, 98–101
    table tops, 108–9
marquetry, faux, 86–7
monochrome colour schemes,
    11
mosaic table tops, 92–5

N

neutral colour schemes, 11

O

office chairs, transformed,
    88–91
oriental bamboo frames, 52–3

P

paint effects
  decorative doors, 136–7
  distressed, 12
  fake marble, 98–101
  faux marquetry, 86–7
  faux inlaid granite, 80–3
  faux malachite, 104–7,
    108–9
  marbling, 108–9
  trompe l'oeil, 62–5, 70–3
  woodgraining, 58–9
  see also stencilling
paper, lampshades, 24–5
pelmets, lambrequin, 112–13
pencil pots, 20–1
photo frames, 20–1
picture frames
  candelabras, 36–7
  fabric, 20–1
  faux malachite, 104–7
  flower vase, 28–9
  oriental bamboo, 52–3
  vinegar painted, 34–5
pillowcases, stencilled, 116–17
pine chairs, stencilled, 74–5
place names, 16–17
plates, painted, 30–1
pots, terracotta, 16–17, 30–1
primary colours, 12

R

rubbish bins, concealing, 70–3

S

screens, windows, 46–7
seating *see* chairs, sofas, stools
secondary colours, 12
seersucker fan blinds, 42–3
sewing box, fabric, 18–19
shelving, tented, 102–3
shutters, clover leaf, 66–7
sleigh beds, 122–3
sofa divans, transforming, 96–7
sofas, covers, 124–7
stencilling
  bedlinen, 116–17
  chairs, 74–5
  faux marquetry, 86–7
  frosted windows, 32–3
  tables, 54–5, 58–9
  trompe l'oeil, 62–5
stools, 76–7
storage *see* cupboards, shelving
Swedish-style
  Gustavian-style cupboards,
    40–1
  Gustavian-style dressing
    tables, 48–50
sleigh beds, 122–3

T

tables
  antique-style consoles, 54–5
  fake inlaid marble, 98–101
  faux inlaid-granite, 80–3
  faux marquetry, 86–7
  marbled, 108–9
  mosaic, 92–5
  stencilled, 58–9
  woodgrained, 58–9
tented effects
  ceilings, 130–2
  shelving, 102–3
terracotta pots, 16–17
  painted, 30–1
tertiary colours, 12
texture, and neutral colours
  schemes, 11
theatre motifs, children's beds,
  128–9
throws
  office chairs, 88–91
  sofa divan, 96–7
tiles
  fake, 133
  fake country, 133
  mosaic table tops, 92–5
tongue and groove cladding, fake,
  130–2
tools, 6–9

trays, finger-painted, 22–3
trellis, fake, 84–5
trompe l'oeil, 62–5, 70–3

V

vases, 140–1
  frames, 28–9
vinegar-painted frames, 34–5
voile drapes, 138–9

W

wardrobes, converting, 40–1
windows
  blinds, 42–3, 50–1
  curtains, 60–1
  pelmets, 112–13
  screens, 46–7
  shutters, 66–7
  stencilled, 32–3
  voile drapes, 138–9
woodgrained and stencilled table
  tops, 58–9

Acknowledgements

My first thank you has to be to my heavenly Father who inspired and guided me with all the ideas and work on this book and answered all my prayers for help often putting talented people in my way who generously shared their ideas and expertise.

I also want to thank the team at Hamlyn, Louise Griffiths who designed the book and Susie Behar who edited text, and to Di Lewis who took all the stunning photographs. Some of the projects in this book were first designed for Charlotte Coward Williams, the Editor of Creative Ideas for the Home whose positive approach and infectuous enthusiasm I am so grateful for. Kirsty Common helped more than she realises in typing and organising my computer.

Thanks too to Tony Lush at Do It All who checked the carpentry projects; to Elaine Green who provided the trellis cupboard idea on page 84; to Myriam Griffiths who contributed the fabric frame and decoupage firescreen on pages 20 and 68, and to Bloomsbury Flowers who added their ideas to mine and made possible the floral tricks on page 140. I owe a debt of thanks too to Mick Flinn at the Stencil Store who over the years has invited me on many of his excellent paint effect courses and to his designer Saleena Khara who provided so much inspiration and help with stencilling.

My thanks too, to all the suppliers listed on pages 142 and 143 whose products made this book look beautiful and whose efforts to manufacture decorating products enriches the lives of so many people.

Thanks too to my husband Andrew and boys Harry and Robert who never once complained of their home looking like a photographic studio.

SUPPLIERS

TEXTILES AND WALLPAPER
Anna French (Tel. 0171 737 6528): lace window dressing on page 138
Baer and Ingram (Tel. 0171 736 6111): wallpaper and fabric page 80
Celia Birtwell (Tel. 0171 221 0877): star fabric on page 17, goblet headed curtains page 60; curtains on page 74; chair cover page 88
Jane Churchill (Tel. 0171 499 9910): kitchen fabric page 11, voile on page 138 and striped voile page 116 and bathroom awning page 130
Laura Ashley: fan blind page 42 and fabric wall page 54
Thomas Dare (Tel. 0171 351 7991): page 10
Crowsons Fabrics: page 126
Do It All (Tel. 0800 436 436): bed linen on pages 114, and 128.
Ikea (Tel. 0181 208 5600): cupboard curtains pages 110.
Malabar Cotton (Tel. 0171 501 4200): page 96
Osbourne & Little (Tel. 0181 675 2255): stool cover page 76, bamboo bedhead page 52
Price & Co (Tel. 01273 421999): Lambrequin pelmet page 112.

Pukka Palace (Tel. 0171 352 5674): page Striped and check voile page 138.
Romo Fabrics (Tel. 0163 750 005): sewing box page 18, fabric screen page 46.
Sandersons (Tel. 0171 584 3344): page 124

DECORATING MATERIALS
Stubbs Hank Designs (Tel. 01543 481211): wrapping paper page 68
AS Handover: gilt leaf on pages 104 and 106

BLANKS TO PAINT
Blankers (Tel. 01404 881 667): swing bin cupboard page 70, frames on pages 28 and 107, table tops on pages 102 and 80.
Decorative Arts (Tel. 0171 371 4303): circular frame page 36
Dormy House (Tel. 01264 365 808): screens on pages 46 and 80
Scumble Goosie (Tel. 01453 731 305): tray page 22, firescreen page 68, tablemats page 104, cupboard page 40, and dressing table page 48, console table Page 54.

STENCILS
Lyn Le Grice (Tel. 01736 364193): page 116
The Stencil Store (Tel. 01923 285 577): soup tureen on page 62 and dining chair page 74
Yes U Can Stencils (Tel. 0171 603 3424): auricula pots page 32, crescent leaves page 48, wood grained table page 58, concealed swing bin cupboard page 70, plates and cups on trompe l' oeil kitchen dresser page 62, and Swedish bed page 122

PAINTS AND GLAZES
Annie Sloan Traditional Paints distributed by Relics (Tel. 01993 704 611)
Colourman Paints (01785 282 799)
Do It All (Tel. 0800 436436): Dulux
Fired Earth (Tel. 01295 814300)
Paint Magic (Tel. 0171 482 6654)
Ray Munn (Tel. 0171 736 9876)
Winsor & Newton (Tel. 0181 427 4343): artists acrylic paints

SPECIALIST MANUFACTURERS
Fleximask masking tape (Tel. 01761 416 034)
Liberon waxes (Tel. 01797 367 555)
Polyvine (Tel. 01454261 276)
Sander Shade (Tel. 01628 529676): Roman blind pages 74–7
Newey (Tel. 01243 379 009): Eyelet kits

FURNITURE AND PROPS
Conran Shop (Tel. 0171 589 7401): accessories page 80
Elephant Furniture (Tel. 0171 243 0203): acessories pages 61, 80, 97and 125
The Pier (Tel. 0171 637 7001): chairs on pages 59, 55, 99, 109 and accessories on pages 67 and 108
Marston Langinger (Tel. 0171 823 6829): chair on page 80 and accessories
Ikea (Tel. 0171 233 2300) furniture on page 74 and 110 and acessories pages on 61, 80, 97and 125

GW00357192

£7.99

ISBN: 978-1-907823-04-6

we love you...

Westie

A 2011 ANNUAL

Written by Rick Glanvill
Designed by Nicky Regan

Contents

8   We Love You ... Westie Because ...

10   Introduction to the Breed

12   Moody and Magnificent

14   Puppies

18   Caring for your Westie ...

21   Spot the Difference

22   The W Factor

24   Highland Bling

28   The Best in your Westie ...

30   Once Upon a Time With the Westie ...

32   Wacky World of Westies

36   International Westcue!

40   Paws for Thought

42   Westies on the Web

46   Go Westie!

48   Woe is my Westie

51   Westie Wordsearch

52   Passport Pooch

54   Real Life Westies

56   World Famous Westies

58   Show the Love

60   Quiz Answers

62   Where's Westie?

... you always play ball.

... you put up with a lot.

... we throw, you fetch.

... you know a thing or two.

... you are so cute.

we love you...

WESTIE because...

... those eyes get us every time.

... you look out for us.

8

... you're our best friend.

INTRODUCTION TO THE BREED

WESTIE FACTFILE

Size:	males 11 inches, females 10 inches
Coat:	double-coated, straight, wiry hair for outer coat
Hair colour:	white
Eyes:	widely set apart, almond shaped, dark brown
Ears:	small, erect, set wide apart
Muzzle:	blunt, a little shorter than skull, powerful
Nose:	black
Tail:	relatively short, carrot-shaped, set high

But anyone who knows them appreciates that it's what goes on in their proud, alert little heads that really stands them apart.

No other dog is quite like a Westie, and no Westie is quite like another.

MOODY &
MAGNIFICENT

Westies punch above their weight in cuteness, intelligence and personality. Physically they are a stocky bundle of white fur broken up with deep, dark eyes and a largish black nose.

Their teeth and mouth are quite large for a dog of this size, and you soon find out why if you don't handle them properly.

Being terriers – bred as sharp-witted hunting dogs – Westies are alert to sudden changes around them and don't waste time before letting everyone know about it. It's why they make great guard dogs (until the intruder sees their size).

Westies actually have two coats. The outer one, which grows to around 2" in length, is wiry and gives the dog its distinctive whiskery appeal. Underneath is its protection against the Highland cold – a short furry layer that hugs the skin and keeps the little fellow warm.

They are not a problem dog as far as health issues are concerned, though there are some problems that regularly crop up – we deal with these elsewhere.

People are often attracted to the personality of a West Highland White as much as its adorable looks, though. They are always on the go, with an alert mind that makes them brave and quite independent, finding their own amusements while always willingly joining in yours.

It's never good to leave them alone to their own devices for too long, mind. Youngsters especially will chew on sight.

If you consider they were also bred to spend a lot of their time chasing vermin down tunnels, you come close to understanding why they are such resourceful little chaps.

These are dogs carrying the remnant of always imagining there's something savage just around the corner, but ready to square up to it.

Despite their origins Westies have a very sunny, friendly disposition for the most part, though owners often report that their family friend had his or her moments of stubbornness, temper tantrums and sulks. They are terriers, after all.

Properly brought up West Highland Terriers should never be yappy or nippy, though. As puppies, especially if you have young children, it's very important to be careful handling them (they're muscular, but only small!) and to discourage them from using their needle-like teeth. An unattended pup can quickly earn a bad reputation.

Older dogs, though, love a bit of rough and tumble and make great playmates for children. If you have other breeds, make sure your Westie doesn't boss them around.

They are strong-willed and do need to be told who is boss very early on. Otherwise you may well find the collar is on the other neck…

With the right guidance West Highland White Terriers are the best friends the family can have – no lapdog, but a loveable, strong little character in their own right.

we love you…

13

It's that irresistible combination: the beautiful white coat and the deep, dark eyes. No, not a mad scientist - the puppy no one can turn away. But is there more to it than seeing and falling in love with a Westie?

Here's our checklist before you buy...

* Research. Amazingly, strong-willed Westies are not everyone's cup of tea. Read up first.

* Reputation. Try to buy from a reputable breeder with good testimonials and accreditation.

* Family. Try to see the puppy with her mother – you'll get a better idea about its health and personality.

* Age. Don't buy a puppy under eight weeks old as they are not old enough to leave their mothers.

* History. Ask to see a history of the dog and its family so you can see it has come from a reputable source.

* Medical. Any puppy should have records of vaccinations, worming and flea treatment. If the pup's pedigree, expect Kennel Club registration papers and details of his parents' treatment too.

PUPPIES

we love you...

AVOID THE PUPPY FARMERS!

The Kennel Club warns against buying from pet shops, dealers or through newspaper or website classified pages. Most, they claim, will have come from puppy farms. 'Puppy farms are like factory farms where dogs are bred purely for profit. The dogs are normally bred too often, many are unhealthy, and often live in unbearably poor conditions.

'The puppies are generally removed from their mothers far too early and sent by rail or van to "dealers" or pet shops in the big cities to satisfy the public's demands. Many are severely traumatised by the transition, and some do not make it alive. Do not buy a puppy or a dog from these sources, as they will have had the worst possible start in life, and are far more likely to have health and temperament problems.'

we love you...

Were you to pick a colour to wear yourself before going for a run around in mud and water all day, the chances are you would not pick white. Poor old Westie – the blessing is also a curse.

For the most part a weekly brush to keep the under-fringe tidy and remove loose hairs will suffice – shedding for this breed of dog is average. Use a short-bristled brush.

Although the Westie's hair makes it a good water dog, it is not a good idea to bathe them – certainly not with any regularity. Part of this terrier's personal armoury is the waterproofing oils produced on its skin. Washing also makes hair lay flat, robbing the little fellow of his or her pride and joy.

If mud has caked on, however, try to let it dry and break, then brush it off. Some people brush through white chalkdust, but this may be damaging to the coat if left in.

In any case you will most likely find that your dog could benefit from professional attention to its coat a few times a year to keep him looking trim and smart. Make sure you use someone who has experience of the breed.

Westies are generally easy to feed but specific allergies prevalent in the breed can lead to skin ailments, such as dermatitis, that will require a change of diet – or home environment, depending on the cause. Seek advice from a vet.

The dog's nails should be trimmed carefully below the 'quick' (the pink part of the nail) every few weeks. If you cannot see the quick, ask a vet for advice. Cutting the quick will lead to bleeding. (If this happens, apply pressure to the area from where the blood is coming until it stops.)

It's also a good idea to brush your dog's teeth and gums (not with your own toothbrush!). The first signs of gum disease can appear around the age of three, and small dogs are more prone to severe problems simply because they live longer (average 15 years).

Try to take your Westie to the vet at least once a year for a health-check, looking for general well-being, worms, any nutritional requirements, or jabs that may need updating. Note also that small dogs wee less and are more prone to bladder problems. They are also more likely to stack on the weight than their larger canine cousins, so be sure not to overfeed.

West Highlands are not a breed that reacts well to being cooped up alone for long periods. They may well develop bad habits and personality traits.

CARING FOR YOUR WESTIE...

Can you spot 10
differences between
these pictures?

Answers on page 60.

SPOT THE DIFFERENCE

THE **W** FACTOR

Westies are not just cute and loyal, they've got talent too. Especially when it comes to singing. We've trawled YouTube for some of the best examples on video, and deliver our verdict on the best and worst Westie divas.

Howl Long Must You Wait For Him?

www.youtube.com/watch?v=gHkjn00Up2M
Unnamed Westie howls along to Coldplay's 'In My Place.' Let's face it, we've all done that. Much worse, probably.
Verdict: WWW – Viva La Diva

Clawsical Music

www.youtube.com/watch?v=JFoP52iK0bs
Clever Clyde Chu punctuates classical piano with some tuneful notes. Obviously a Westie with some singing pedigree.
Verdict: WWW - Johann Sebastian Bark

A Night At The Operooo

www.youtube.com/watch?v=dvpUJXnkCzw
Marvellous Molly delivers a polished accompaniment to 'Un Bel Di Vedremo' from Madame Butterfly.
Next up: 'La Bowoweme.'
Verdict: WWW - Pawverotti

Losing the Lead in Phantom

www.youtube.com/watch?v=Ln7BqlwwvyA

Kute Kiche can't get enough of 'Phantom Of The Opera' it seems. Calling Lord Lloyd-Webber – great new idea for a TV audition show …

Verdict: WWW - Raouuuuul

Which Voice is the Dog's?

www.youtube.com/watch?v=1da1KN6IUpE

Perfectionist Paddy carries an ol' time music hall tune better than his warbling owner. Simon Cowell might ask you back – but on your own.

Verdict: WWW - Black Eyed Poochie

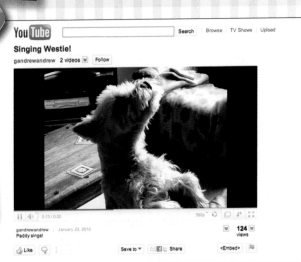

But we have a winner...

Soap Operatics

www.youtube.com/watch?v=BvSaeeUUH-o

Fourteen-year-old crooner Scamp waits like a seasoned session musician for the moment to join in the 'Coronation Street' theme. And it's just like Frank Sinatra from there on.

Verdict: WWW – SuBo-ne

HIGHLAND BLING

How far would you go to dress your Westie to impress? These days there are plenty of companies supplying designer gear for canines. Some of the stuff almost serves a purpose!

For a small fee Puchi Petwear will add your Westie's name in lights (well, 1cm high diamante) to his or her collar. They call it 'Pimp My Name Collar' of course.

Pimp My Name Letters (DCO359)

£2.00 Inc VAT

These sparkling diamante letters are designed for the "Pimp My Name Collar," they simply slide onto the patent strap. Available in clear diamante.

Size: 1cm in height. Price per letter.

Pimp My Name Personalised Dog Collar (DCO358)

£15.00 Inc VAT

Pimp your dog's name with this fantastic personalised collar! Available in sizes 7"-14" neck in a pink or black strap. (Letters are sold separately) *Please note these collars are for decorative use only and should not be attached to a lead*

Images: Puchi Petwear

Talk to the Paw Dog T-shirt (DOC322)

£18.00 Inc VAT

This fabulous tee will make any dog glam! With diamante detailing for extra sparkle! Available in pink or baby blue. Available in sizes Small-Superdog

Rainbow Dog Cardigan (DOC482)

£25.00 Inc VAT

Stripes are soooo this season - just look on the street - and this rainbow of humbug toffee shades is just the height of urban autumnal chic. Zips up across tummy. Comes with gorgeous silk padded hanger.

As featured on "This Morning" (ITV)

Available in sizes XSmall (toy breeds) - XL (Spaniel size)

All prices subject to change

Paris Velour Dog Hoodie (DOC463)

£19.99 Inc VAT

These fab new hoodies are perfect for snuggling your pooch in! Made from the softest velour, and with a diamante Puchi 'P' they are sure to catch the eye of any fashion-conscious pooch! Available in sizes Small-Superdog.

Waffle Dog Harness and Lead in Purple (HAR475)

£19.99 Inc VAT

The must-have colour for this season! This fantastic soft harness will keep your dog comfortable on a walk. Made from breathable waffle material and with protective lining, complete with a matching lead. Available in rose pink, purple and baby blue.

25

we ♥ love you...

26

Your Westie is not a fussy eater as such, but the poor things are prone to allergies and other ailments that can be avoided with a little care and attention.

Try to feed your Westie the best quality dog food you can afford as these are balanced properly for their size. Never leave the food out in the bowl longer than 30 minutes. If she has left it she is probably full.

Treat her with most raw fruit and crunchy vegetables, especially cut apples and whole carrots.

There is quite a long list of foodstuffs that are not generally advisable to give your Westie. However, these are only guidelines and should by no means be taken as definitive.

Avoid...

Most table food, especially rich or fatty meals which can create digestive problems.

Chicken, turkey, fish and pork bones – they can splinter and stick in the throat or cause internal damage.

Sweet cakes or bread dough – the dog's heat can make dough rise in its stomach.

Some breeders warn against wheat, corn and soy in the diet because of possible allergies.

Onions as they may cause anaemia in dogs.

Alcohol, raisins, grapes, avocadoes and mushrooms, which are all toxic to Westies.

Anything containing caffeine, and chocolate, which has the stimulant theobromine in it. These can overstimulate the heart muscle and trouble the nervous system.

Oh, and don't leave used food bags or foil lying around as these may give a greedy Westie serious internal damage.

THE BEST IN YOUR WESTIE...

Tradition has it that the 'earth dogges' that James I (also James VI of Scotland) demanded be sent from Argyllshire on his arrival in London were ancestors of today's West Highlands. Even such royal patronage did not immediately mean they caught on as household pets, though.

The first Westies were white-furred pups selected from rough-coated terrier stock and bred for their whiteness. The idea of keeping them as pets really took off in the Edwardian era.

'No breed has made more swift a swoop upon popularity than the West Highland White Terrier,' enthused the 'Illustrated London News' in July 1913. 'Unknown except in the wildest parts of the Highlands [it] came south one year, attacked the shows with a startling vigour of entries, and fought its way into the recognition of a separate place in the Kennel Club Register with most surprising suddenness.

'In 1906 no one dreamed of its invasion: the conquest began in February 1907, with a skirmish upon "Cruft's" where 49 entries in five classes unmasked the strength of the breed.'

By October of that year, the ILN notes, the Cruft's entries for Westies numbered 83. Oddly, since the West Highland was a renowned hunter of badgers as well as otters, Cruft's categorised the breed as 'non-sporting dogs'!

By May 1913, 326 hopefuls were entered for the show – a record for any terrier, and the Westie never looked back. The individual names included 'Kilree Bag O' Tricks', 'Walpole Winter', 'Scotia Chief' and 'Swaites Cruachan'.

Amazingly, Westies were more usually employed for otter hunting in the 1910s because they 'stand wetting and hard work much better than any fox terrier,' as one Scots pack master put it at the time.

Otter hunting would traditionally run from Shrovetide to Midsummer and was said to be beloved of English royalty since King John. Queen Elizabeth I's Master of the Otter Hounds was paid a princely salary of £13 6s 8d a year.

Victorian owners of trout fisheries encouraged the sport to limit the hungry otters' meals, but opinion was divided in more modern times. Not on grounds of morality, you understand.

'Half the sporting world regard the pursuit of Lutra Vulgaris as little better than a glorified rat hunt,' suggested 'The Times' in 1911, 'while the other half share Venator's opinion that "it is much pleasanter than any other chase whatsoever".'

Otter hunting was banned in England in 1979 and Scotland in 1982. Now that otters have been reintroduced to wild parts of Britain with some success, it may be as well to keep your Westie away from those areas in case instinct – and ancestral memory – takes over.

ONCE UPON A TIME WITH THE WESTIE...

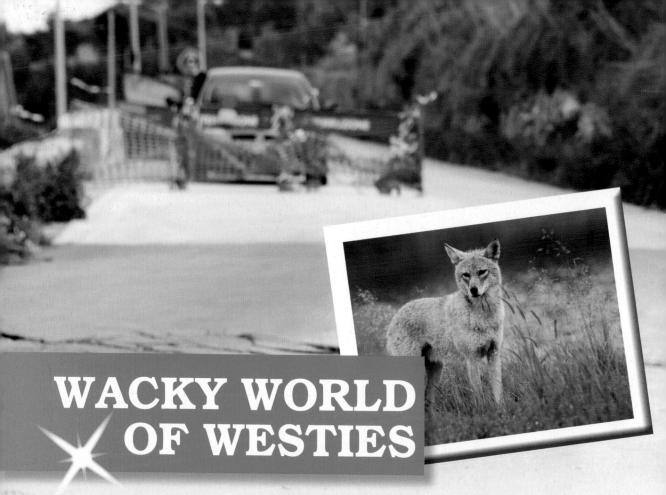

WACKY WORLD OF WESTIES

FELINE UNWELL

Snowy the Westie, from Huntingdon, managed what some of her friends merely dream of doing: she hunted down and ate five cats – whole. In summer 2010 Snowy was rushed off to the medic unable to hold down any regular food, and it was only after associate vet Carol Barker carried out a routine x-ray that the truth was revealed: inside the dog's stomach was a family of five toy ceramic moggies, each one to two inches long.

NOSTRA-PAW-MUS

In June 2010, Thomas, a twelve-and-a-half-year-old Westie foresaw possible doom in Ottawa, Canada. His owner Joy Headland was sick with worry when he refused to come for his usual shopping trip for the first time in his life – he loves car journeys. Was he ill? Reluctantly, Joy went by herself – and promptly found herself in the middle of an earthquake. She raced home expecting Thomas to be as petrified as she was. But the prescient pooch seemed delighted with himself for staying at home. Next up: Thomas predicts the winners of the Ashes series, UK Election, and Cruft's.

SOUTH PAW

Barry the Westie, seven years old at the time, was at his usual post in Brooker Creek Preserve, Florida, USA back in March 2009. He had taken it upon himself to protect the family home from wild critters – whether the family wanted him to or not. In the past he had come out on top in a battle with a pygmy rattlesnake. But he was lucky to survive when a coyote – which really should be in a different weight division altogether (30lbs compared to the terrier's 20lbs) – got the better of him with bites on the neck, spine and wedding tackle. Happily, after a patch-up, Barry returned to his station, vigilant as ever.

Rosie, The New School, Exeter

YES, EXMINSTER

The head of The New School, Exminster, Devon, found a loveable eleven-year-old Westie in a local dogs' refuge in 2008 and adopted her for the private school for three-to-seven-year-olds. There were, of course, concerns about health and safety in the classroom and Ofsted were called in. You might expect the schools inspector to wash their hands of the matter. In fact, as long as the children did the hand-washing after touching her, they were happy for Rosie to hang around.

LONGITUDE AND LAPDOGITUDE

A 'Dog Map of Britain' (yes, that does just say 'dog') produced in 2008 revealed that the part of Britain with highest per capita rate of 'handbag dogs' was the north-west of England. But Scotland had the best taste: according to their figures there were more Westies north of the border than anywhere else in the country.

CANDY-COATED

A lorry driver once drove 200 miles to return a lost Westie. Way back in July 1958, Candy, an inquisitive eleven-month-old pup, strayed from her family's home in Oaklands, Hertfordshire, onto nearby woodland. She was picked up later by a kindly truck driver who saw her weaving in and out of busy traffic on the A1. Thirteen-year-old Jean Tilley found out about the rescue and cleverly posted an advert in the lorry drivers' mag, 'Headlight.' George Holmes, 29, got the message and drove all the way from his home in Leeds to put Candy back with her folks. What a sweet man.

PAWS FOR THOUGHT

we love you...

Just 5 minutes longer ....

Don't even think about it!

Chicken!

Capital Paws
www.capitalpaws.com/fun

Some very funny Westie-centred humour on this US website. We particularly recognised the home truths behind the spoof in their 'Westie Property Laws' –

1. If I like it, it's mine.

2. If it's in my mouth, it's mine.

3. If I can take it from you, it's mine.

4. If I had it a little while ago, it's still mine.

5. If it's mine, it must never appear to be yours in any way.

6. If I'm chewing something up, all the pieces are mine.

7. If it just looks like mine, it's mine.

8. If I saw it first, it's mine.

9. If you are playing with something and you put it down, it automatically becomes mine.

10. If it's broken, it's yours.

Westie Savvy
www.westiesavvy.com

A commercial UK website (training videos promoted) that's made much more interesting by its regular new blog entries. Some are videos of cute puppies being trained, but elsewhere there are articles posted about every aspect of the dog with a lively community of Westie fans offering their own advice and tips.

Find A Puppy
www.the-kennel-club.org.uk/services/public/psar/buy/find/puppy/West+Highland+White+Terrier.findapuppy

They really should come up with a snappier web address than the current finger-strainer, but the Kennel Club's online service allows you to click on your local area and find a list of breeders with puppies registered with them. Not all are Accredited Breeders, although Find A Puppy does indicate which are, and can also alert you when the area list changes.

Westie Names Database
www.westhighlandwhite.co.uk/namesdb

If you're looking for inspiration for a name for your soon-to-arrive Highland chap, here's a great place to start. Hundreds of names of Westies have been submitted over the years and faithfully recorded here. Ones we liked: Goliath, Quincy. Not so much: Ogden, Timotheus.

WESTIES ON THE WEB

West Highland White Terriers have some of the most extensive coverage in digital media. Here's our selection of some on the World Wide Westie.

Breed Clubs

If you fancy you have a potential Westie of the Year, there are plenty of shows to enter right across Britain. Most of the websites offer basic breed information and contacts as well as dates of upcoming shows.

Scotland
www.thewesthighland
whiteterrierclub.co.uk

North of Ireland
www.northofireland
westhighlandwhite
terrierclub.co.uk

England
www.thewest
highland
whiteterrierclubof
england.co.uk

Midlands
www.midlandcounties
blackandwhiteterrier.
co.uk/index.html

South
www.southernwesthighland
whiteterrierclub.co.uk

we *love* you...

It's maddening when you spend half the day travelling somewhere and when you get there dogs are strictly verboten. Here's our guide to some of the best places in the UK that say 'We love Westies'.

Balloch Castle Country Park, West Dumbartonshire, Scotland

Set within Loch Lomond Regional Park, one of Scotland's areas of 'national scenic significance,' with a wonderful old castle in good nick and gardens that sweep down to the Loch itself.

Goodrington Sands, nr Paignton, Devon

Dogs are welcomed all year round on the north side of this gorgeous expanse of beach, which also has plenty of pubs, golf and activities for children nearby.

Slapton Sands, nr Torcross, Devon

Dogs can enjoy the incredible beaches here for 12 months of the year. Plenty of history too: the huge rolling sand dunes were used secretly in preparations for the Normandy Landings in WWII.

Daymer Bay, nr Wadebridge, Cornwall

Does your Westie surf? We only ask because Daymer Bay, where dogs are welcomed all year, is one of Britain's great centres for wave-riding. There are no bins for scooped poop, though, so be prepared.

Watergate Bay, nr Newquay, Cornwall

Set on the wild north coast of Cornwall, this is a vast expanse of beach perfect for long walks, but with plenty for young humans to do too.

GO WESTIE!

we love you...

Grizedale Forest Park, Cumbria

Let your Westie experience the arts in the wild with this ancient woodlands walk with the occasional public sculpture to stop and admire.

Beachey Head, nr Eastbourne, Sussex

Even the most distracted dog might appreciate the extraordinary sea views from the famous Sussex cliff top paths between East Dean and Birling Gap. Play safe with a short lead, though, and never let Westie go near the edge.

Fernilee Reservoir, nr Whaley Bridge, Derbyshire

In the heart of the Peak District National Park, a wonderful walk past reservoirs packed with sailing boats, and the dam on the Goyt River, followed by a woodland stroll.

Wombwell Woods, Wombwell, Yorkshire

An inspiring walk for nature-lovers through ancient broadleaf woodlands with many different types of butterfly and bird visible – or audible – including skylarks.

Cherwell Valley, nr Upper Heyford, Oxfordshire

How about a cool waterside walk along the Oxford Canal and River Cherwell? Plenty of wildlife along the route, and no need to use a lead for long stretches.

Newborough Forest, Anglesey, Wales

A three-hour circular walk around the former Druids' refuge, taking in sandy expanses, grassy mounds and ancient lighthouses.

MEDICAL COSTS

West Highland Whites are generally regarded as a low-risk pet as far as medical costs are concerned. However, that does not mean any one individual won't run up huge vet's fees. A dog accidentally swallowing something that won't budge, for example, might run into a four-figure sum and have you howling.

Rather than pay a monthly premium, some owners set aside a small amount in a savings account to cover the unexpected.

In pet insurance terms Westies are at the bottom end of the price range compared to larger dogs, and younger ones come at a lower premium too. There are plenty of very good insurers out there, but always read the policy thoroughly before making your choice.

ALLERGIES

The most typical of the common problems that West Highland Whites suffer more than most breeds are related to allergies.

'Westie skin' – 'atopic dermatitis' – leads to bald areas, and red itchy patches that can drive your poor pooch to distraction. It usually reveals itself when Westie is aged six months to three years.

The first step if you suspect this is to have a vet verify the condition, and eliminate food allergies or parasites, before suggesting clinical treatments of the skin problems directly.

Some owners believe in different courses of further action to help relieve the irritation. A change of diet can help, removing bacteria and any likely allergens. Some swear by natural self-help, especially herbal oils (eg aloe vera or calendula), sometimes in shampoos. Some homeopathically-trained vets also prescribe vitamin and

Steroids have sometimes been used to clear skin complaints, but used long-term these may have nasty side-effects.

CONJUNCTIVITIS

We've all seen this in children, when the membrane of the eye that produces mucous becomes inflamed and red. Unfortunately Westie is the breed most susceptible to Kerato Conjunctivitis Sicca, a similar problem, where the eye dries up through lack of lubrication and the cornea might become damaged. If you suspect this is happening, contact a vet straight away.

DEAFNESS

We might think she's just cocking a deaf-'un out of sheer bloody-mindedness, but Westies are genuinely predisposed to loss of hearing. It's congenital and not just a 'terrier' thing – breeds as diverse as the miniature poodle and great dane are in the firing line. There is little that can be done medically for a deaf dog, but you will have to be extra careful to avoid accidents or surprises for your loved one – especially out walking and if children are around.

SICK SINUS SYNDROME

Older Westies are prone to abnormal heartbeats, leading to lack of breath and fainting, a condition known as Sick Sinus Syndrome. In some cases a pacemaker can be fitted to regulate the heart, but most vets recommend tablets to reduce the seizures.

PREVENTION

Never forget Westies are hunting dogs with bundles of energy. They need good walks, companionship, the sun on their backs, a properly balanced diet and regular loving care from their owners. A well Westie is a happy Westie!

WOE IS MY WESTIE

We never like to think about it, but sometimes Westie is in the wars – and won't he let us know about it. Here we look at some of the health issues you might want to think about.

49

we love you...

Westie Wordsearch

There are 12 words associated with Westies mixed up in the grid below. They go horizontally, vertically and diagonally in all eight directions. Can you spot them all? Answers on page 60.

B	G	N	I	N	I	A	R	T	Z
L	R	G	L	N	X	E	X	L	W
D	F	E	H	A	I	P	T	U	E
N	P	V	E	R	Y	B	A	F	S
A	W	U	R	D	A	O	I	Y	T
L	W	E	P	R	I	H	L	A	I
H	T	W	K	P	S	N	M	L	E
G	X	R	Z	A	Y	X	G	P	T
I	T	R	E	W	H	I	T	E	F
H	Y	L	D	M	T	R	P	V	C

Bark
Breeding
Highland
Leash
Loyal
Playful
Puppy
Tail
Terrier
Training
Westie
White

PASSPORT POOCH

If you want to take your Westie on a European jaunt with you, you have to get him a dog passport first.

The EU's Pet Travel Scheme (PETS) now means that no quarantine period is required on returning to the UK from EU countries.

It is a time-consuming process making him travel-worthy, so make sure you plan well in advance.

Your local vet will be able to direct you to your nearest government-authorised Local Veterinary Inspector (LVI). This is the only person who can provide your dog with a passport (PETS documentation) from the Department for Environment, Food and Rural Affairs (Defra).

The LVI will only issue the passport if you arrive there with the following:

- Your Westie - microchipped. It must be fitted with a microchip by your vet so that it can be identified (do this first of all).

- Documentation of a vaccination against rabies. Your vet should record the following on the documentation:

  - Dog's date of birth/age.

  - The microchip number, date of insertion and location of the microchip on the animal.

  - The date of vaccination.

  - The vaccine product name.

  - The batch number.

  - The date its booster vaccination is due (calculated by reference to the vaccine manufacturer's data sheet).

  - Proof of a blood test. In most cases the vet should carry this out to ensure that the vaccine has worked.

Be aware that you will almost certainly have to wait for 21 days to elapse from the vaccination date before attempting to travel to the continent.

You will also need to have booster jabs within six months of the vaccination, or blood test if applicable. If you miss the booster you have to start again from scratch.

Should your wanderlust fill up the dog's passport, you simply have to revisit the LVI and obtain a new one. Take Westie and the passport along too.

Travelling further afield with your dog is more complicated. Check the Defra website - www.defra.gov.uk/wildlife-pets/pets/travel/pets/index.htm – or ring their helpline on 08459 33 55 77.

REAL LIFE
WESTIES
BY THE SKED
FAMILY,
EDINBURGH

Before we got
Jezz lots of
people used
to tell us that
Westies don't
have a very
nice nature,
don't train well
and aren't very
lively...

we love you...

we love you...

JEZZLE'S STORY

Jezzle's Favourite Things

- Walks
- Gravy bones (treats)
- Eating roasted meat
- Playing fetch the slipper
- Sleeping
- Being cuddled
- Going in the sea
- Shredding tennis balls
- Barking at cats

... but Jezz has a lovely nature and was very easy to train. He also loves to play and is great around people. We couldn't have asked for a better family pet!

Jezzle is a very sociable dog and is always eager to greet other dogs whilst on his walks. One of his favourite games as a puppy was to cling onto larger dogs' tails and hold on for as long as possible.

Training Jezzle was a great experience and lots of fun. We took him to a puppy training class where he made lots of great friends. Every Monday night we went along and learnt all about the training process and, within a few weeks, he was sitting, staying, lying and walking to heel like a professional. I discovered the key to a dog's heart at the training classes - love, care and, of course, food! Now, every night he gets a gravy bone which is his favourite treat, and he barks for it.

Jezzle is an extraordinary dog. I don't know what our family would do without him. I feel we have become more active since purchasing a pup and I also think it gives our family a lot more time to bond.

Jezzle loves relaxing. All in all, he is a very pampered pooch. As you can see from the pictures, he loves having long naps and resting after walks.

Jezzy can't drive, but he sure loves car trips. Sometimes he gets to sit on the front seat.

Jezz is very cheeky sometimes, like the time he stole a sausage right off the barbeque. Too bad it was too hot to eat!

Even though Jezz occasionally misbehaves, overall he is a super pet who proves the saying 'A dog is a man's best friend' is very true indeed.

PUPPY LOVE

In 2008 the world's most expensive living artist, American Jeff Koons, unveiled a 12.3m tall model of a West Highland White Terrier called Puppy, whose skin entirely comprised flowering plants. It currently stands guard outside the Guggenheim Museum in Bilbao, Spain. 'Puppy has a lot to do with fertility,' Koons claimed. 'It functions as the life and death cycle. Birds and bees are fertilising the flowers. There's something coming into its peak – the flowers bloom – then a decline into death sets in.' We think he just loves Westies.

POSTAL SERVICE

This 1979 stamp is one of a set of four issued by the United Kingdom post office. The other British breeds were Welsh Springer Spaniel, Old English Sheepdog, and Irish Setter. Hold it – aren't *they* supposed to lick *us*?

CARRY ON, MACINTOSH

A spoilt brat West Highland Terrier called MacIntosh made his literary bow in Pelham Grenville Wodehouse's 'Very Good Jeeves' and became the frequent bane of brainless Bertie's life. MacIntosh's owner, domineering Aunt Agatha, far prefers pooch to nephew, but regularly requires Wooster and Jeeves to dogsit, with hilarious results.

Maggie, Cesar's Westie

HAIL, CESAR!

When Mars Inc. spotted the trend that dog-lovers were switching to smaller breeds they launched a 'leading edge of nutrition' brand to cater for the growing market: Cesar (pronounced like Caesar, by the way, not as in the Spanish name, César). Naturally they opted for a West Highlander to front up their fashionable product.

LAMENTABLE

Wee Jock is the tiny law-keeping sidekick of BBC's 'wild west of Scotland' detective, Hamish Macbeth (played by Robert Carlyle). Unfortunately stardom was short-lived for the first Wee Jock – he was killed by escaped convicts in the fifth programme of series one, called 'Wee Jock's Lament'. The Westie who played the original Wee Jock was called Zippy. Later ones were simply called Jock.

TOO WHISKY

Strange to think that the Scotch whisky so beloved of the Rat Pack in the 1950s started life as the 'House of Commons' blend of Buchanan and co of London in 1884. However, common usage – 'the one with the black bottle and white label, please guv' – soon prompted a name change and what better way to reflect the new 'Black And White' than with a 'blend' of two terriers: a West Highland White and a Scottish Highland Black.

HOUSE TRAINED

Hugh Laurie, who played Bertie Wooster in one TV adaptation of 'Jeeves And Wooster,' briefly 'adopts' a Westie in the US TV hit, 'House' (season three, episode 21). The dog, Hector, chews up his belongings overnight, but by the time the real owner returns to reclaim him, House has inevitably fallen for Hector's Westie ways and is sad to see him go.

You can't blame creative types for seeing Westies as the perfect pooches to win over the public. So here's a selection of the most famous in popular culture.

WORLD FAMOUS WESTIES

WEST HIGHLAND SHORTBREAD

FUR FIGHTERS

Westies are synonymous with Scotland in many advertisers' eyes. The brand identifier of 3m's 'Scotch Fur Fighter' hair remover is a Westie, and he smiles winningly on the front page of their website at www.3m.com/brands/scotch/furfighter.

PROFESSIONAL PEEK

Mr Peek and Mr Frean started up their south-east London biscuit business back in 1857, their motto being 'a guarantee of purity'. Naturally, they chose Westies to grace the iconic packaging of their famous West Highland Shortbread, a success story that helped Bermondsey become known as 'Biscuit-town.'

'BLACK & WHITE'

SCOTCH WHISKY

'BUCHANAN'S'

FESTIVE WESTIE

Noel is a great name for one of our West Highland chums, don't you think? It's also a good time of year to spread the love of them. Happily there are Christmas card packs with cute Westies under the tree, standing on a snowy doorstep, watching the baubles alongside a cat (well trained, that one). We especially like the one in a floppy Santa hat.

W: thewestieshop.designsales.co.uk

WEST END PUPS

When 'top people's store' Harrod's is stocking, you know you're in good company. The Knightsbridge store has a range of Westie-adorned products, from umbrellas to shopping bags, but for a fraction of the cost you can nab one of their chintzy Westie purse key rings. That little touch of glamour every time you open the door after a walk.

W: www.harrods.com

UPWARDLY MOBILE

What does everyone need to stop themselves looking silly while shouting down their mobile phone in public places? Why, something that shows they actually have taste. Pedigree Charm have small encrusted Swarovski crystal Westie charms, pink or clear. They can also hang from a key ring or school bag, of course.

W: www.pedigreecharm.co.uk

EBAY GUM

The online marketplace eBay has hundreds of Westie-related products for sale at any given time. We found various ancient ceramics, Royal Crown Derby paperweights, watches, plushes and tax disc holders. But our favourite was a 1930s wall plaque bearing the legend: 'He asks me no questions he tells me no lies and when I address him looks straight in my eyes. Content with a little he never despairs but in all my troubles he willingly shares. He asks me so little he gives me so much then always let sympathy dwell in my touch.' (Sob.)

W: www.ebay.co.uk

It's sometimes difficult to avoid becoming a little, shall we say, obsessed, with Westies. What the hell, though. It's much more fun to fill your house with terrier-ware than Simpsons scatter cushions. See what you think of this kitsch kollection.

SHOW THE LOVE

Quiz answers

P21 SPOT THE DIFFERENCE

P51 WORDSEARCH

60

we ♥ love you...

61